D0105602

THE
JOURNEY

Also by Alister McGrath

The Unknown God: Searching for Spiritual Fulfillment
Christian Spirituality: An Introduction
J. I. Packer: A Biography
Christian Theology: An Introduction
A Passion for Truth
Beyond the Quiet Time

THE
JOURNEY

A Pilgrim

in the Lands

of the Spirit

A l i s t e r M c G r a t h

Doubleday

New York   London   Toronto   Sydney   Auckland

PUBLISHED BY DOUBLEDAY
a division of Random House, Inc.
1540 Broadway, New York, New York 10036

DOUBLEDAY and the portrayal of an anchor with a dolphin are registered
trademarks of Doubleday, a division of Random House, Inc.

Book design by Patrice Fodero Sheridan

First published in the United Kingdom by Hodder & Stoughton Limited

Library of Congress Cataloging-in-Publication Data

McGrath, Alister E., 1953–
The journey: a pilgrim in the lands of the spirit / Alister McGrath.
        p.   cm.
Includes bibliographical references.
I. Spiritual life—Christianity.   I. Title.
BV4501.2.M23575   2000
248.4—dc21   99-36568
                                                       CIP

ISBN 0-385-49588-9

Copyright © 1999 by Alister McGrath

All Rights Reserved

Printed in the United States of America

June 2000

First Edition in the United States of America

1   3   5   7   9   10   8   6   4   2

Contents

Introduction

We are all on a journey, whether we like it or not. For some, that journey leads from birth to death and no further. For others, who have come to know God, that journey is more complex. Those two basic road markers of human life remain in place. Yet they are supplemented by others and are seen in a different light.

Life is now seen as an anticipation of something more marvelous that is yet to come. Death remains yet is no longer to be feared. It is to be seen as the removal of the final barrier between the believer and the rapturous encounter with the living God. This book is about this journey of faith, and the ways in which we can draw closer to God before we finally meet Him face-to-face. It is perhaps the greatest journey that can ever be undertaken and brings immense satisfaction and fulfillment to those who make it. But it is also difficult, challenging, and perplexing. Those who travel need constant encouragement and reassurance from those who have undertaken the journey before them.

For many, that journey begins with a sense of dissatisfaction. There has to be more that we know to life. We sense that somewhere over the horizon there is something as yet unknown that will offer us the spiritual satisfaction and fulfillment that has thus far eluded us. It is like an early explorer, convinced that new worlds lie beyond the horizon, who will not be satisfied until he has discovered and explored them. To encounter God is to begin a new way of life so radical that we could speak of "being born again."

For others, the journey has already begun. Some have loved God ever since they were capable of loving anything. Others have grown up within a Christian environment and absorbed its ideas and values. For such people, the journey is that of deeper exploration into something they already possess—yet do not fully understand or appreciate. The journey promises to be rewarding in that they are aware that there is much more to their faith than they have yet grasped.

Many Christians are unaware of the riches their faith has to offer. Jesus compared the kingdom of heaven to a pearl of great price—something that was worth selling everything for. The possession of this pearl brought a satisfaction that was without parallel. Yet for most of us, the kingdom of heaven is more like the reference manual that comes with a new piece of equipment—something complicated and dull. We feel we ought to know more about it but rather hope that we can get by with what we already know.

There is something wrong here. The problem does not lie with the Christian faith. Christianity does indeed offer us a priceless pearl, something of enormous intrinsic value and worth. The problem is that this pearl has been thrown before swine like us, who just don't appreciate its wonder and joy. We have failed to grasp its beauty and comprehend its value. Many of those who think that they are dissatisfied with Christianity are really dissatisfied with something else—their own grasp of Christianity. For most of us, we have scraped the surface and nothing more, yet we mistakenly believe our superficial encounter represents the gospel in its totality.

This book is about digging deeper. It is written for people who are tired of too-easy ways of approaching the Christian faith. For many of us, our engagement with the Christian faith is somewhat superficial. At least, that is what I found about my own faith. I had given much time to trying to understand the basic ideas of the Christian faith and appreciating the wonderful way in which those ideas interlock. I had gained a lot from grasping the wonderful coherence of Christian doctrine.

Yet, at times, this seemed to be little more than just kicking ideas around. It was as if there were one part of my life that dealt with ideas, and this somehow never seemed to come into contact with anything else. It began to seem unreal and irrelevant. As I wrestled with this, I began to realize that my faith was actually quite superficial. I had *understood* things, but had failed to *appreciate* them. I had not made the connections that would have led to the enrichment of my faith and the deepening of my spiritual life. Quite simply, I had missed out on some of the great riches of the faith. As I began to discover them, I found myself wishing that I had encountered them long before. Then I began to do some serious reading and reflection. It took me ten years to sort myself out, but it was worth it.

This book is written for people like myself—people who want to dig deeper and explore further and are fed up with being given trite and shallow answers to the big problems of Christian living by well-meaning pastors and friends.

My hope is that this work will help others who are dissatisfied with their grasp of their faith and who want to do something about it. The first step in getting things right is to have a framework for understanding the Christian faith. This gives us a way of making sense of what we are doing and where we are going. It allows us to visualize our situation so that we can identify the problems and get them sorted out.

The framework this book offers is not the only way of thinking about the Christian life; nevertheless, it is one that countless Christians have found invaluable down the ages. The image? A journey. This book invites you to join me as I reflect on how we can keep going and keep growing on that journey.

But first we need to set the scene for this journey. . . .

1

PREPARING FOR
THE JOURNEY

Chapter I

The Journey

The Bible is saturated with the image of a journey. Wherever we turn, we read of individuals making journeys. Perhaps the greatest of those was the forty-year journey of the people of Israel from their harsh captivity in Egypt to the Promised Land of Canaan. Elsewhere, we read of Abraham stepping out in faith to leave the land of his ancestors and go to a place chosen by God. He did not know where he was going, but he knew whom he would be traveling with, and that was good enough for him.

We also read of pilgrims setting out to travel to Jerusalem, daunted by the thought of the mountains they must climb and the harsh conditions they will face, and yet consoled by the thought of the presence of God as they travel. We read of the people of Jerusalem returning home after their long period of exile in Babylon. The New Testament relates how the earliest term used to refer to Christians was "those who belong to the

Way" (Acts 9:2). They were to be seen as travelers on their way
to the New Jerusalem.

Thinking of the Christian life as a journey through the world
offers us a vivid and helpful way of visualizing the life of faith.
Consider each of the following points.

1. The image of a journey reminds us that we are *going somewhere.* We are on our way to the New Jerusalem. It encourages us to think ahead and look forward with anticipation
   to the joy of arrival. One day we shall finally be with God,
   and see our Lord face-to-face!
2. Traveling does more than lead us to the goal of our
   journeying. A journey is itself a process that enables us to
   grow and develop as we press on to our goal.

To travel is thus about finally achieving journey's end, with all the
joy and delight that this will bring—but it is also about inducing
personal and spiritual growth within us as we travel. Journeying is
thus a process that catalyzes our development as people and as
believers.

This is an important point and needs to be considered further.

JOURNEYING AND SPIRITUAL DEVELOPMENT

In one sense, people who complete the journey are the same as
when they began it. Yet in another sense, they are different in that
they have been changed by what they experience. A journey is a

process of personal development, not simply a means of getting from A to B. To travel to a distant land is a purposeful and intentional matter. We must believe that this journey is worth undertaking. The journey itself offers us the chance to deepen our commitment to its object. As we journey, we have the opportunity of reflecting on our goal and anticipating our arrival.

Anticipation of the joy of reaching that goal then becomes a means of sustaining us as we travel. Spiritual writers of the Middle Ages used the Latin word *viator* to refer to a believer. The word literally means "a wayfarer" or "a traveler"—someone who is passing through the world. The term points to the need to see oneself as a traveler, not a settler; someone who is passing through the world, not one who expects or wants to remain there.

The journey also allows us to understand ourselves better. Each of us is a complex mixture of strengths and weaknesses, some of which are known to us and others that are hidden from us. Those strengths can help us minister to others and build up God's kingdom, just as those weaknesses can hinder us. Learning about ourselves, and responding to what we find, is an important aspect of Christian discipleship. To journey on our own is to have the time and space to uncover ourselves; to travel with others is to allow them to identify the strengths and weaknesses we manage to hide from ourselves, and be supported as we try to engage with them.

Yet the Christian life is not easy, nor is it meant to be. Jesus himself pointed out that following in his footsteps involved taking up a cross. To be a Christian is potentially to suffer. As Christians down the ages have discovered, the quality of Christian witness is directly proportional to the extent to which the church is persecuted. Even in happier times the life of faith can be painful and discouraging.

Sometimes the difficulty arises through false expectations, raised by well-meaning evangelists or pastors who tell their followers that becoming a Christian guarantees health, wealth, and happiness. More commonly, we get discouraged because we feel that God is distant or unreal, or that we are not capable of sustaining our faith throughout the journey that lies ahead. What we thought would be a brisk and brief stroll turns into a marathon for which we are simply not properly prepared.

It is at this point that the theme of "spirituality" comes in. Nowadays, everybody seems to realize how important spirituality is. Spirituality is all about the way in which we encounter and experience God and the transformation of our consciousness and our lives as a result of that encounter and experience. Spirituality is about the *internalization of our faith*. It means allowing our faith to saturate every aspect of our lives, infecting and affecting our thinking, feeling, and living.

Nobody can doubt how much we need to deepen the quality of our Christian lives and experience, with God's gracious assistance, and live more authentic lives in which we experience to the full the wonder of the love and grace of God. We need to get in training for the marathon that lies ahead. It all sounds so simple and easy—in theory. In practice, however, things are not quite so straightforward.

So what hope is there for people like me, then, who aren't very good at spirituality? How are we going to manage to get further along the road of faith, when we find that we are already stumbling and weary despite our best intentions? The beginnings of an answer lie at hand. We need to pause, gather our thoughts, and plan for the remainder of the journey of faith.

✤ PAUSING FOR THOUGHT

The journey has already begun.

That's why we start thinking about it.

These two statements may strike some readers as odd. Yet most of us begin to realize the importance of preparing for this journey only once we are well under way in the life of faith. In the neat and organized world many of us would prefer to inhabit, it wouldn't be like that. The life of faith would be planned with military precision. It would be like the Allied plans for the invasion of Europe in 1944. A huge amount of planning would go into the operation. Every last detail would be sorted out. Provision would be made for every contingency.

Yet the real world is much more untidy than these idealists appreciate! Most of us set out on the journey of faith not fully comprehending the implications of what we have done. It's only when we've started that we realize we should have laid the groundwork properly. So what do we do then? Give up? Certainly not!

The best preparations are made once the journey is under way.

Does that strike you as strange? It may seem ridiculous to talk about laying the groundwork for the journey after you have begun. On reflection, though, it makes a lot of sense. Until we realize what the problems are, we can't prepare for them properly. Experience of being on the road helps us make provision for the challenges that we now know lie ahead. At first we didn't; now we do. So let's adjust and get on with it.

Imagine that it is a hot summer day and you decide to walk for miles along dry and dusty roads to visit a famous landmark. You set out with great enthusiasm at dawn for the journey. You look forward to seeing the sights along the way. You are impatient to reach your final objective, which you have been told is *really* worth seeing. So you head off in a great burst of enthusiasm, not bothering to take any water. Who needs that? You don't bother to make sure you have certain basic skills—like being able to read a map. Nor do you take any protection against the glare of the sun. Maybe others need those—but not you!

The first ten minutes are great. After an hour, you begin to tire. After two hours, your mouth is dry and you are thirsty. The sun is getting higher in the sky, and you know that the heat is soon going to be unbearable. After three hours, you grind to a halt. You know you are not going to make it to the end of the road. In fact, you're not even sure where you are. You were sure you wouldn't need a map. Anyway, you wouldn't have been able to read it even if you have taken one with you.

So what are you going to do? When all is said and done, you have two options. Here's the first.

You can give up. You can tell yourself that you've been stupid and unrealistic and go home. You're wiser than when you started out. Yes, you ought to have known. Yes, you should have prepared properly for the journey. But you just didn't realize it was going to be that tough.

But you don't need to do that. There's another way of coping that is much more effective and that keeps you on the road. Here's the second option.

You take a break. You know that you've not prepared properly. But you also know that you want to keep going. This time, you know the difficulties you'll encounter. So you stop off at the next town along the way and buy a map, some bottles of water, some protection against the sun, and you recover your strength. You ask someone to show you where you are on the map and how to read it. Then you start off again. This time, you'll make it.

Think of this as a new phase in the journey. You aren't giving up. Quite the reverse, in fact. You are making sure that the next phase in the journey will succeed because you've acquired the skills and resources that you now realize you need. You could say that the first was your naive phase, and the second your mature phase. Or perhaps you could think of the first as the simplistic and the second as the reflective phase.

But whatever terms you use, the point is the same. You learn as you journey. You learn what you need—and then you learn how to get it. You can pick up those skills and resources on the way.

This book is written for those who are on that journey and have discovered their lack of readiness. It aims to show how we can keep going on that journey and learn to cope and grow as we travel.

Some of those difficulties can be anticipated. Tiredness and opposition are among the more predictable difficulties we shall encounter. But others perhaps take us by surprise. The despair of doubt has to be tasted before its power to destroy can be realized. Our human nature, upon which we rely so heavily, proves to be inadequate. Our spirit may be willing, but our flesh is weak (Matthew 26:41).

Was it not Peter who vowed to stand by and defend his Lord,

come what may? Then, under the pressure of fear, he denied even knowing the man. His resolve to be firm was real; it simply crumbled under the reality of stress. In the Bible, failure is so often the key to success. It is when we fail that we realize that we have trusted in a false divinity—usually our own strength and wisdom!—and are moved to rediscover the one in whose strength and wisdom we were meant to trust all along.

At this point, the wise pause to think. Where fools give up in the face of unexpected difficulties, the wise see these as opportunities to learn and develop. Tomorrow is the day on which we shall begin the journey again—but this time properly prepared.

So how do we prepare? Let's think about images and themes.

❧ IMAGES, NARRATIVES, AND THEMES

Western Christianity has been deeply affected by a particular way of thinking, a way of thinking that has seriously limited our grasp of our faith and apprehension of its wonder. Many call it "the Enlightenment"—the period in Western culture that began about 1750 and placed enormous emphasis on the power of human reason. Reason could explain everything.

It was inevitable that Christians would be affected by this way of thinking. Its basic demand is this: Understand better! Advancement in the Christian life takes place through a deepened understanding of the basics of Christian teachings and a deeper knowledge of the biblical works. This demand to read, learn, and understand has undoubtedly been helpful in many ways. For a start, it leads to better-informed Christians with a much better grasp of the basic Christian beliefs.

Yet in another way, it had led to spiritual impoverishment.

Why?

The emphasis on reason has been at the expense of our *imaginations* and *emotions*—two God-given faculties that are meant to be fully involved in our Christian life. Spirituality is about linking thought, imagination, and feeling as we appreciate the full richness and depth of our faith. *The gospel does not just affect the way we think; it changes the way we experience the world.*

For the first period of my Christian life, I thought Christian development was all about thinking harder about things I already knew. It brought some useful results. For example, I realized how important it was to explain key Christian ideas faithfully and effectively, and I developed several ways of doing this that have proved very helpful to others. But it soon became obvious that this had its limits. I stalled. It was as if my faith were affecting only a tiny part of my life.

It was then that I began to realize the importance of letting biblical ideas impact on my imagination and experience. I read some words of a medieval writer whose name I continue to have difficulty in pronouncing. Geert Zerbolt van Zutphen (1367–1400) stressed the importance of meditating on Scripture. *Not understanding, but meditating.* Here is what he had to say.

Meditation is the process in which you diligently turn over in your heart whatever you have read or heard, earnestly reflecting upon it and thus enkindling your affections in some particular manner, or enlightening your understanding.

These words brought new light and life to my reading of the Bible. I had thought that meditation was some kind of Buddhist practice that was off limits for Christians. Yet I had failed to notice how often Old Testament writers spoke of meditating on God's law. Meditation was about letting the biblical text impact upon me, "enkindling the emotions"—what a wonderful phrase!—and "enlightening the understanding." And my heart, as well as my mind, was to be involved! The worlds of understanding and emotion were brought together, opening the door to a far more authentic and satisfying way of living out the Christian life.

I also began to explore the theme of *projecting oneself into the biblical narrative.* In other words, when Scripture recounts what happens, allow yourself to be caught up in that narrative. Up to this point, I had thought that what we were meant to do was to increase our factual knowledge of events. For example, when reading a text about the ministry of Jesus in Galilee, it was important to be able to find Galilee on a map, understand its cultural history, see how this fitted into the general pattern of Jesus' ministry, and even try to date the event.

Yet this led to nothing more than the accumulation of facts. It did not excite or challenge me. If I am being honest—and here I know I speak for countless unfortunate Christians—it even managed to make reading the gospels a little dull. What was meant to be inspiring and wonderful became little more than a history lesson. Something was wrong—maybe with me, but certainly with the method I was using and had been encouraged to use.

Let me make it clear that I had, and have, not the slightest difficulty with the idea of the total trustworthiness and reliability of Scripture. My faith is securely grounded on the two unshakable rocks of Jesus Christ and Scripture. The problem was that I seemed to be engaging only with a small part of a much greater whole. There was more to the Bible than I had grasped. The problem lay with the deficient way I was reading Scripture, which treated it as little more than a series of factual statements.

Then I encountered an alternative, another way of engaging with the gospel accounts of the life and death of Jesus. Christians had been using it for centuries; it was just that I hadn't come across it. I found this approach set out very clearly in a late medieval writer I had been working on in connection with a research project, Ludolf of Saxony. Here is what Ludolf had to say about reading the gospel accounts of the life of Jesus:

> *Be there with the angel, like another witness, at the moment of the holy conception, and rejoice with the Virgin Mother now with child for you. Be present at his birth and circumcision, like a faithful guardian, with St. Joseph. Go with the Wise Men to Bethlehem and adore the little king. Help his parents carry the child and present him in the Temple. Alongside the apostles, accompany the Good Shepherd as he performs his miracles. With his blessed mother and St. John, be there at his death, to have compassion on him and to grieve with him. Touch his body with a kind of devout curiosity, handling one by one the wounds of your Savior who has died for you. With Mary Magdalene seek the risen Christ until you are found worthy to find him. Look with wonder at his ascent into heaven as though you were standing among his disciples on the Mount of Olives.*

I had to think of myself as being there, witnessing what is said and done. I began to read the gospel narratives with new excitement. The mental effort I had to make to "project" myself into the biblical world meant that I appreciated what I found all the more. Ludolf forced me to stand beside various key actors in the biblical narrative and join them as the drama of human redemption unfolded in front of their eyes—and mine.

My life of prayer was immeasurably enriched by this procedure. No longer was I simply registering ideas as I read. I was reliving the historical events on which my faith was grounded. Meditating on the biblical text led to my entering into the world it described. Ludolf explains the general principles of his approach as follows:

> *If you want to draw fruit from these [gospel scenes], you must offer yourself as if present to what was said and done through our Lord Jesus Christ with the whole affective power of your mind, with loving care, with lingering delight, thus laying aside all other worries and care. Hear and see these things being narrated, as though you were hearing with your own ears and seeing with your own eyes, for these things are most sweet to him who thinks on them with desire, and even more so to him who tastes them. And although many of these are narrated as past events, you must meditate on them all as though they were happening in the present moment, because in this way you will certainly taste a greater sweetness. Read then of what has been done as though they were happening now. Bring before your eyes past actions as though they were present.*

I found that I knew exactly what Ludolf meant when he talked about using "the whole affective power of your mind, with loving care, with lingering delight." Meditating in this way on the gospel text led naturally to an enhanced appreciation of all that Jesus is and all that he had done for me. It led most naturally into prayer.

Reading the Bible leads to meditating on the Bible, which leads to praying from the Bible.

This sequence of events gave structure and purpose to my engagement with God through the Bible. I found myself both understanding and appreciating some words of Guigo II, the noted medieval spiritual writer:

Reading without meditation is barren.

Meditation without reading is prone to error.

Prayer without meditation is lukewarm.

Engaging with the Bible was thus about far more than just reading and understanding; it was about allowing every aspect of my life to be transformed by the text so that I could turn to God in prayer.

So what did I learn from this? A number of things, some of which lie behind the distinctive approach of this book. Here are the three most important.

1. When dealing with a biblical *image*, it is essential to pause and allow the passage to generate a mental picture. We have to enter into the world of that image. We need to project ourselves into the image and become part of it, experiencing its richness and implications.

2. When dealing with a gospel *story*, we must enter into it, standing alongside those who witnessed the savior of the

world. We need to meditate on these gospel narratives as though they were happening in the present moment.

3. When dealing with a biblical *idea* or *theme*, it is not enough to understand it. It needs to be applied to our lives so that it becomes a lived reality rather than an abstract and lifeless notion. Christianity is not simply about ideas; it is about the transformation of spiritual reality.

An example may make this third point clearer. Take a simple idea: forgiveness. We can all understand this. But that is not enough. *We need to experience the reality to which that word points.* It is fatally easy to think that we have "understood" the word without entering into the real world of experience and life to which it refers. "Forgiveness" is what restores a relationship that really matters when you have messed it up. It is about the restoration of something that means everything to you and that you thought you lost forever on account of your foolishness.

If you have ever been through that situation, the word "forgiveness" will mean the transformation of your life, evoking powerful emotions and calling to mind the situation that made it necessary. Someone who has never needed to be forgiven will never know the full richness, wonder, and joy of that simple word "forgiveness."

Perhaps these brief statements will not be enough to explain fully what I have in mind. However, it will become clear in the second part of this work, as we put them into practice.

But our thoughts return to the journey. How will we cope with it? What resources are available? In what follows, we shall begin to explore a major theme lying behind this book—that others have made that journey before us.

Chapter 2

A Map for the Journey

Only a fool would undertake a journey without some idea of where it might lead—and how to get there. The question of how to get from A to B is one of the most basic issues of life. Travelers long ago mapped out the best routes from Egypt to Canaan, or from Babylon to Jerusalem. Looking at the map allowed the traveler to work out how much farther he had to journey.

But how did that map come into being? At its heart, a map is the distillation of the experience of travelers—those who have journeyed in the past and recorded their memories in the form of pictures and symbols. The map represents the cumulative wisdom of generations of travelers, put together for the benefit of those now wishing to make that same journey.

To undertake a journey with a map is therefore to rely on the wisdom of the past. It is to benefit from the hard-won knowledge of those who have explored the unknown and braved danger in order to serve those who will follow in their footsteps. Behind the lines and symbols of the map lie countless personal stories—stories the map itself can never tell. Yet sometimes those stories need to be told, just as the hard-won insights of coping with traveling can encourage, inspire, and assist us.

THE EXODUS

One of the greatest journeys in the world was that made by the people of Israel, who left behind the bondage of Egypt as they set out for the Promised Land. It is a powerful and deeply moving story that mingles hope and despair, faith and doubt. It is a story that continues to inspire some four thousand years after the events it describes.

It is easy to draw a map that shows Israel's journey from Egypt to the Promised Land of Canaan. The map shows well the physical obstacles that Israel encountered—the Red Sea, the desert, the mountains, and the rivers.

What this map does not show is the deeper journey that went alongside the physical journey. For Israel did more than travel from Egypt to Canaan. It had to discover its identity as the people of God and the responsibilities this brought.

If it were possible to draw such a map, it would have to depict this deeper journey. The physical barriers would be supplemented by spiritual ones—such as doubting God's love and care, yielding to temptation, and turning away from what God wants us to possess in favor of some lesser goal. We still face those obstacles on our journey of faith.

The biblical account of the Exodus can be read in several

ways. We can read that story as an account of a great event in the past. There can be no doubt that the events described happened or that they established the identity of the people of Israel. To recount the events of the Exodus—as Jews still do at the feast of Passover—is to call to mind the origins of Israel and its divine mission to the world.

Yet that is not the only way in which that story can be read. Once we begin to see the story of the Exodus in this light, it comes to have a deeper significance and power that illuminates our situation.

The Exodus tells our story.

Each of us has a personal journey to make, from our own Egypt to our promised land. We have left something behind in order to make this journey. We have had to break free from our former lives in order to begin afresh. *We* were in Egypt. *We* were delivered from bondage. *We* are in the wilderness, on our way to the promised land. The story of the Exodus *involves* us—because it is *about* us. We can therefore enter into that narrative knowing that it is our story. We belong in it, and it belongs to us. It is all part of the history of our redemption, of which we are part.

This book is an invitation to use the framework of the journey from Egypt to the Promised Land to make sense of the personal pilgrimage of faith. Yet this is not a journey that need— or should—be undertaken alone. Fellow travelers, past and present, are part of the gracious provision of God by which he enables us to achieve what he purposes.

❧ REMEMBERING AND ANTICIPATING

Imagine . . .

You are on a road. It stretches far into the distance, before you and behind you, before disappearing over the horizon. As you make your way along this long and often lonely road, you may find yourself wondering what lies beyond the horizon. With this thought, we come to one of the great themes of Christian spirituality—*remembering and anticipating*. It is a way of thinking that helps us to keep going along that road.

Earlier, we began to think about the deliverance from Egypt and the important role this played for the people of God. It helped them get their spiritual bearings. As Israel journeyed, it looked back with relief on its deliverance and forward with expectation to its future entry into the Promised Land.

The Exodus led from Egypt to the Promised Land through the wilderness. The period of wandering in the wilderness was seen as a time of preparation—a period in which Israel could discover more about itself and the God who loved, called, and liberated it. Israel's long period of wandering in the wilderness was no easy time. At points, it was a time of doubt, rebellion, and restlessness. Yet, at others, it proved to be a time of dedication and purification, a period in which Israel was able to discover her identity as a people and the reasons for being called into existence by the Lord.

As Israel wandered in the wilderness, it was constantly urged to look backward and forward. It looked *backward* to the past and recalled its period of captivity in Egypt and its glorious liberation through Moses. It looked *forward* to the final entry into the Promised Land, the eagerly awaited goal of Israel's long journey. The present was thus sustained by the memory of past events and the hope of future events.

The themes of "remembering" and "anticipating" play a pivotal role in the Old Testament understanding of the Exodus. Israel is constantly reminded to remember its exile in Egypt and recall all that God has done for it since then (Psalm 135:5–14; Psalm 136:1–26).

A similar theme emerges during the captivity of Jerusalem in Babylon during the sixth century before Christ. The familiar words of Psalm 137 capture the sense of longing felt by the exiles for their homeland:

By the rivers of Babylon we sat and wept
When we remembered Zion.

The thought of returning to the homeland sustained the exiles throughout the long and harsh years of exile. It can also sustain us today. For we are exiles on earth, cut off from our homeland on account of sin, who look forward eagerly to returning to the heavenly realms.

The Christian life is thus poised between past and future. The journey of faith is sustained by *memory* on the one hand and *anticipation* on the other. Israel looked back to its deliverance from Egypt and remembered the faithfulness of the God who had called it into being. It looked ahead with an eager hope to the final entry into the land that flowed with milk and honey. As Israel struggled through the wilderness, these were anchors that secured faith in times of doubt.

Living between the times, poised in the present in that most delicate interplay of past and future, is no easy matter. It is like the trapeze artist who lets go of the security of one bar and soars through the air, poised to catch the next support. Each of the trapeze bars offers security; yet for a moment, the artist is not supported by anything. She is suspended between her securities, caught in an act of faith. The Christian life on earth is like those midair moments, moments of uncertainty and risk that are finally resolved only when we take hold of what lies ahead of us and grasp it securely and irreversibly.

The Christian is thus invited to remember and anticipate. The past and the future break into our present life of faith, enfolding it as an alpine valley is embraced by the mountains on either side. In the past, we remember the great act of redemption in which God delivered us from sin, death, and despair through the cross and resurrection of Jesus Christ. And in the future, we anticipate the final entry into the New Jerusalem, to be with God forever and luxuriate in his holy, kindly, and caring presence.

So how does this help us as we travel along that road of faith? How can we apply this theme to our situation?

Imagine that you have been a prisoner of war. You have spent many years far from your loved ones and are longing to see them again. The war has ended, and you have been liberated. You can go home! You have been told that your loved ones are alive and well and that they are longing to see you. You are wondering what they will look like after all those years. You can't wait to be reunited.

But you have to wait. There is a shortage of transport, and you will have to walk to meet them. It will be a long walk. It will be like the inhabitants of Jerusalem returning to their homeland after many years of exile in Babylon. And you are not looking forward to the journey even though you long passionately to reach its promised goal.

Two things will help you cope with that long and arduous journey.

First, think about what you are leaving behind. The captivity; the squalor; the pain and hopelessness. The more you think about these, the more you will want to leave these behind.

Second, think about what lies ahead. Imagine that you are walking up the steps of the old, familiar house. You are walking toward the door. It is thrown open, and the longed-for joyful faces greet you again. You begin to savor the delight of homecoming—greeting old friends, revisiting familiar places, and being welcomed back into the warmth of your family.

The pattern of reflection that underlies Christian spirituality can thus be summarized like this:

- *remembering* all that God has done in the past;
- *anticipating* all that God has promised to do in the future;
- *resolving* to deepen the quality of our Christian faith and life in the present.

The present is thus a moment in which we can recall with gratitude what God has already done for us and look forward with confident expectation to what he will do. These thoughts reinforce us, reassure us, and propel us into the future with a new determination to do all we humanly can to deepen the quality of our faith.

Yet there is another aspect of traveling that we need to consider. We are not meant to travel alone. How can others help us? We shall consider this in the next chapter.

Chapter 3

Hitchhiking on the Road of Faith

The journey is long and tiring. Its final goal is entry into the Promised Land. What greater excitement could there be?

Yet there are few who have not experienced the weariness of traveling along that road. Its milestones are tinged with tears and sweat. Sometimes that road seems endless, at other times pointless. There will be moments when we sit down by its side in dejection, wondering why we ever bothered setting out in the first place. It is a long and lonely road. There is nobody on it to listen to our sorrows and console us.

Most of us think thoughts like that every now and then. But there is another thought that needs to be set alongside them, which allows us to see our journey in a new light. *Others have made the same journey before us.* They have experienced its highs and lows firsthand. They developed ways of coping with the tiredness, cynicism, and downright waywardness they knew on that journey. Its milestones are stained with their tears. And some of them

have passed on their experiences and insights to those who follow. We are not alone; we are surrounded by a cloud of witnesses
(Hebrews 12:1–2) who are shouting their encouragement and
advice to us as we struggle onward.

So how can we make the best use of this wisdom—wisdom
that has been quarried from the living stone of past lives of faith
and tested on the journey of faith?

One answer is to hitchhike, to get a ride with others who are
much better at this kind of thing than we are. In what follows, we
will explore this helpful image and see how it casts light on the
resources available to us for the Christian journey.

⟡ THE HITCHHIKER

One of the most enduring symbols of the popular culture of the
1960s and 1970s is the "hitchhiker," reflected in the titles of
books such as Douglas Adams's *The Hitchhiker's Guide to the Galaxy.*
The hitchhiker was someone without a care in the world, who
wandered around the world by hitching rides with friendly truck
drivers. It is an image that is immensely helpful to Christian
spirituality, as it reminds us that we do not have to be alone or
depend on our own resources as we journey. There is another
option open to us. We can hitch a ride with someone else.

To hitchhike is to get a free ride and travel in company. By the
end of our ride, we are farther along the road than when we
started, and we have enjoyed company along the way. To hitch a
ride is to learn more about people and life as well as move along
the road to our destination. It is to learn from the wisdom of
others, who accompany us for a while along the road before

dropping us off. We can then rest and reflect by the side of the road before hitching another ride with someone else.

I have found this image enormously helpful as I have tried to deepen my own grasp of the Christian faith. To be quite honest, I am lousy at prayer and personal meditation. I realize that they are important. It is just that I don't seem to be very good at them. I admit that I need help here in a big way. Yet one of the great themes of Christian faith is that we do not have to journey on our own. We are not the only ones on the road of the Christian life, nor are we the first ever to have made that journey. In his grace, God provides others who can help and sustain us, allowing us to draw on their strength as we hitch a ride along the road to the New Jerusalem.

All of us need to face up to our limitations. I can't write music like Mozart. In fact, I can't even play Mozart's music. Yet I feel uplifted and moved when I hear someone else play his music. Someone else is able to ennoble me by doing something that I just couldn't do for myself. I can't paint like Rembrandt. As a matter of fact, I even have difficulty painting my bathroom door. Yet I find Rembrandt's pictures deeply inspiring, moving me to reflect more deeply on the meaning of life and history. I may be lousy at something, but there are others who are much better and from whom I can try to learn.

In much the same way, I am not much good at praying. Yet when I read the prayers of someone like Augustine or Luther, I find myself being deeply moved by what they say. Somehow, they are able to help me to help myself. Now, isn't this what the "body of Christ" is all about? Each of the parts of the body has its own distinctive role to play. Not all of us are good at every-thing. But through God's good grace, there are people around who can help us do things that we aren't good at. They are there to help us, and they are meant to be used as we travel along the road of life.

To hitch a ride with the great spiritual writers and thinkers of the past is to learn and be encouraged. They set out—sometimes long ago—on the same journey of faith. Through reading and reflecting on their writings, we can travel alongside them, absorbing their wisdom, on the one hand, and taking great comfort from the fact that they chose to undertake the same walk of faith as ourselves. The ideas they developed arose from a lifetime of wrestling with the rich resources of the Christian faith and the realities of the spiritual life. Their efforts are to our benefit. We can absorb the wisdom of a lifetime as we walk along with them. When the time comes for us to move on, we find that we have learned from their ideas and examples and been encouraged and affirmed by their presence with us as we travel.

This book, then, is about a journey. But it is not a journey we have to make on our own. Others have made this journey before us and have left us encouragement and guidance so that we may follow them. We could think of them as having drawn maps based on their own experience and insights, which we can use to navigate. So important is this basic idea that it needs to be explored further, using another image. Having looked at the image of the hitchhiker, we now turn to an older and less familiar image—that of the rutter.

✦ THE RUTTER

The sixteenth century was an era of exploration on an unprecedented scale. Following the discovery of the Americas in 1492, many European nations set out to explore the known world, mapping new routes to hitherto unknown regions. The secrets of the seaways of the world were being opened up as routes to Asia were discovered and carefully recorded. The Portuguese navigators unlocked the secrets of the Strait of Magellan and the Cape of Good Hope and established new trading routes to the rich markets of Asia. The captains of these voyages of discovery became national heroes in Spain, Portugal, and England.

Yet these voyages of discovery were undertaken at great cost. The seaways to the New World destroyed many who had hoped to conquer them. Those who returned had learned the secrets of the routes and recorded them in a small book—the rutter. Rutters were the key to the secrets of the world's seaways and the best hope for a captain who wished to return home alive.

A rutter was basically a book in which the ship's pilot recorded every detail of the voyage so that his steps could be retraced in safety. It related exactly how he got to his objective and how he returned home. The rutter was priceless because it contained the detailed navigational records of someone who had been there and lived to tell others of what he found and how he got there. The rutter related how the pilot had steered for so many days on such and such a bearing and what he had encountered along the way. The location of dangerous shoals, the bearings of landmarks such as headlands, the depths of channels, the location of safe harbors—all were meticulously recorded. Anyone getting hold of these rutters would be able to retrace the steps of those who had been there before and gain access to the riches that lay ahead.

It is no wonder that the rutters for the trade routes to Asia from Europe were classed as secret by the Spanish and Portuguese. Some were written in code; others included deliberate errors known only to their authors, designed to mislead those who were not meant to have access to their secrets. Those who hoped to be guided to the new worlds thus found themselves lured onto hidden rocks and destroyed. But a reliable rutter was the key to a safe voyage to the secret lands beyond the horizons.

The rutter was thus a powerful amalgam of expertise and personal experience on the part of its author. It did not aim to offer a complete chart of the oceans of the world but simply to ensure that one specific route could be traveled safely. Those who followed their author could do so in the knowledge that he had been there before them and passed down his hard-won knowledge. The voyage ahead would be long and difficult. Yet it helped those making it enormously to know that someone had successfully completed it before them *and* that he had passed on to them a detailed notebook of how he achieved it. A rutter is thus more than a map. It mingles geography with personal experience, explaining how the journey was made so that others can do the same.

A physical rutter pointed out rocks and other such dangers; it also identified safe harbors and sources of food and water. Spiritual rutters allow us to identify some of the main difficulties we may encounter along the road of faith so that we may make good use of strategies that others have devised before us. They help us find spiritual refreshment and safety and offer us a vision of our final arrival at our destination.

We need to be clear about something before we go any further. Nobody is saying that being a Christian is just about replicating what other Christians have thought and done. Each life of faith is completely original and is grounded in the unique identity of each believer. Every rutter reflects the personal experience of a unique individual. There is much that we can learn from those who have been there before us. But in the end, we have to get on with the real business of the Christian life and not just read books about what other people thought and did. We can filter their insights through the lens of our own lives and allow them to come to focus on our personal journey of faith.

Yet nobody can make this journey on our behalf, as some kind of proxy. There are no surrogates in the life of faith. We need to undertake it ourselves, while being encouraged and enlightened by those who have gone before. It is up to us personally to assimilate and make our own the wisdom of others. So let us prepare to step out in our imaginations and build up a mental picture that will help us make sense of the great journey that lies before us. We shall be making use of understanding, imagination, and emotion as we aim to appreciate the full wonder of the gospel and allow it to sustain and encourage us as we travel.

We need to be able to picture in our minds the spiritual landmarks along the way, the obstacles we shall meet, the safe havens where we may shelter, sources of food and water, and— above all!—the destination that is our goal. This book aims to draw on the rutters of those who have been there before us and who wait for us to join them with eager anticipation.

2

THE JOURNEY THROUGH THE WILDERNESS

In this book, we shall be allowing the Exodus to be a framework for making sense of the Christian life and helping us to understand both what is happening to us and what we can do to improve the quality of the life of faith. We can think in terms of this improvement having two different elements.

First, there is the objective aspect of the life of faith—namely, our relationship with God. What is there that we can do to deepen our commitment to God and our understanding of what he wants us to be and do?

Second, there is the subjective aspect of that life, namely, the way in which we experience the walk of faith. What can we do to enhance the quality of our experience of God and cause us to yearn passionately to be with him? How can we allow our emotions to deepen our love for God and appreciate all the more what he has done for us in Christ?

The story of the Exodus, as we have seen, is not just about past events—ancient history that has no impact on us today. It is part of the living history of the people of God and relates an experience that embraces us today. The Exodus took the people of Israel from the land of Egypt through the wilderness to the Promised Land and can guide and encourage us today as we make that journey from bondage to freedom and finally enter into the promised inheritance that awaits us.

We shall divide this journey into four stages, each of which moves us further along the road of faith. Each of these four stages involves reflection on three major themes:

1. *A Landmark.* These give structure to the journey, helping us to understand where we are going and orient ourselves on the road of life.
2. *A Wilderness.* This is when the going gets tough and we feel dry, exhausted, and discouraged. We need to get through these feelings, knowing that we will emerge as stronger people when we do. But we need encouragement if we are to cope with them and keep moving along.
3. *An Oasis.* These are the parts of the journey that breathe new life into our weary souls. Here we experience refreshment and renewal and can recharge our resources for the next part of the journey.

Thinking of these three will give structure to our thoughts, as we continue on the journey ahead of us. We need to know where we are, where we are going, what the difficulties will be, and the resources at our disposal to help us cope with them. And we need to mobilize all our God-given faculties—understanding, will, and emotions—as we engage with the challenges that lie ahead.

And so we prepare for the first stage of our journey. . . .

Chapter 4

The First Stage

When Israel came out of Egypt, its faith was strong. God had led it out of the land of captivity with signs and wonders. There was no reason to doubt his presence or power. The pillar of cloud led Israel by day, and the pillar of fire by night. It was easy to believe and trust in God. After all, God had liberated Israel from captivity and would soon lead its people into the Promised Land, flowing with milk and honey.

Yet, as Egypt receded into the distance, the harsh realities of the journey through the wilderness began to take priority. Egypt was just a memory. The Promised Land lay somewhere in the future. The present was dominated by the grim reality of the harsh and inhospitable wilderness.

There was no other way to the Promised Land. As the New Testament makes clear, there is no glory without suffering, no resurrection without a cross. There is no cheap entry into the

New Jerusalem, no quick fix to get into the Promised Land. We must journey onward, traveling in hope.

So what thoughts might guide us as we travel? We turn to our first landmark. . . .

✒ LANDMARK: CREATION

One of the great landmarks of the Christian faith is that the God we know and love is the creator of the world. Yet so often this is just an idea we accept. It must become a landmark on our personal journey of faith, impacting on our hearts as much as on our minds. It needs to transform our consciousness and lives. So let's allow that to happen. We'll begin by looking at how it transformed the outlook of some weary and dejected people long, long ago and far, far away. . . .

In the sixth century before Christ, many of the people of Jerusalem were in exile in Babylon. They longed to return home. One of their concerns was that God had forgotten them. Or perhaps he was powerless to save them. It was to those anxious people that these words were spoken (Isaiah 40:26–29):

> Lift your eyes and look to the heavens:
> Who created all these?
> He who brings out the starry host one by one,
> And calls them each by name.
> Because of his great power and strength
> Not one of them is missing.
> Why do you say, O Jacob, and complain, O Israel,

"My way is hidden from the Lord
My cause is disregarded by my God"?
Do you not know?
Have you not heard?
The Lord is the everlasting God,
The Creator of the ends of the earth.
He will not grow tired or weary.

These words are of considerable importance. Note how the doctrine of creation is related directly to the human situation. As we journey, we naturally wonder whether God knows about us—or cares for us. The doctrine of creation is here seen as a reassuring landmark. We need to pause and consider the following points in a little more detail. Let each of these points impact on you and savor the point that is being made.

First, notice the appeal to the starry heaven. The point being made is that each star has been created by God. Each is special; each is named by God. He forgets and overlooks none. The doctrine of creation reminds us that God cares for all that he has created. Yet humanity is the height of God's creation! We are created just a little lower than the angels (Psalm 8). If God cares this much for aspects of his creation, how much more will he care for us! Creation is an affirmation of the love and care of God for those he brought into being.

Now apply this insight. Don't just *think* it; apply it. What difference does it make? How does it help you to quicken your pace as you travel? Here is one way of applying it.

Look around you.

What do you see? Everything that you observe has been made by God. The God who has called you is the God who has made this world, through which you are passing. Is not he greater than anything in this world? Will not the one who made all things see you through all things as you journey to be with him? The doctrine of creation is thus enormously reassuring.

When I was young, we used to sing a children's hymn that goes like this:

God who made the earth
The moon, the sky, the sea;
Who gave the light its birth
Careth for me.

It's a very simple hymn, but it's a wonderful insight. The God who made everything that we can see, and more besides, cares for us. *We matter to him.*

Second, creation reminds us of the grandeur and splendor of God. The God whom we know and love is the God who brought everything into being. As we pass through this world, we can see it as the personal handiwork of a personal God. His wisdom, power, and love is reflected in its sights. For the people of Jerusalem exiled in Babylon all those years ago, this was a thrilling insight. Why?

Let's enter into their situation and experience their sadness and bewilderment at their fate. A great new empire had arisen and had overwhelmed the people of God. Was this the end? And where was God in all this? It must have seemed to many that God had lost touch with things and that events had spiraled out of control.

So what use is the doctrine of creation? What does it have to say in this distressing situation? Isaiah 40:6–8 offers us an answer. The empires of the world will come and go, but God remains forever. The transience of the great world powers is contrasted with the permanence of God.

> All men are like grass
> And their glory is like the flowers of the field.
> The grass withers and the flowers fall
> Because the breath of the Lord blows on them.
> Surely the people are grass.
> The grass withers and the flowers fall,
> But the word of our God stands forever.

This gives us a new perspective on the doubts and bewilderment we so often experience on our journey through life. The God who made the world will outlast the waywardness of any aspect of his creation.

Look around you. Where is the Assyrian Empire? Or the Babylonian? Or the Roman Empire? Or the British Empire? Or the Soviet Empire? All these great empires have been like the flowers of the field. They were great and splendid in their day. Maybe they cherished the idea that they would last forever. Yet they faded away like grass in the hot sun. Only God endures forever, to support and sustain those who trust in him.

So what else are we to make of this landmark? We now turn to hitch our first ride on our journey. . . .

Hitching a Ride: **Jonathan Edwards**

Jonathan Edwards was born at East Windsor, Connecticut, on October 5, 1703. In September 1716 Edwards entered Yale College, New Haven (now Yale University), where he later served as a tutor from 1724 to 1726. When he was around seventeen years of age, Edwards underwent a conversion experience. As he read I Timothy 1:17, he was overwhelmed by a sense of God's greatness and glory. "As I read the words," he wrote later in his personal journal, "there came into my soul, and it was, as it were, diffused through it, a sense of the glory of the divine Being; a new sense quite different from anything I ever experienced before."

In 1726 Edwards resigned his post at Yale in order to become a pastor in the little town of Northampton, in Massachusetts. Here, Edwards would see a renewal break out in the winter of 1734–35. The "Great Awakening," as it came to be known, had a major impact on North American Christianity. Edwards later moved to minister to a congregation at Stockbridge, where relatively light parish duties allowed him to write a series of major theological works that continue to be widely read and valued. His reputation as a scholar firmly established, in 1757 Edwards was invited to become president of the College of New Jersey, Princeton (now Princeton University). Following an unsuccessful inoculation against smallpox, he died at Princeton on March 22, 1758, and is buried in the local cemetery.

Edwards is a remarkably vivid and powerful writer whose works continue to excite and encourage Christians. So what would Edwards want us to gain from him as he accompanies us along the way?

One of Edwards's most compelling works is a sermon entitled "The Christian Pilgrim." In this sermon, Edwards is concerned to help us orient ourselves correctly as we travel along the road of faith. As we pass through the world, what should be our attitude toward it?

Because it is God's creation, we cannot reject it as evil. Yet because it is not God, it falls short of the true glory of the ultimate goal of our journey. Edwards reminds us that our final goal is God and that nothing else has the power to satisfy or right to be adored other than that same God. Edwards here declares that "God is the highest good of the reasonable creature; and the enjoyment of him is the only happiness with which our souls can be satisfied." We may therefore pass through the world and enjoy all that it has to offer, while realizing that the final delight of being with God will totally overwhelm whatever joy and delights this world may offer.

If Edwards were to walk alongside us, this is what he would say.

We ought not to rest in the world and its enjoyments, but should desire heaven. . . . We ought above all things to desire a heavenly happiness; to be with God; and well with Jesus Christ. Though surrounded with outward enjoyments, and settled in families with desirable friends and relations; though we have companions whose society is delightful, and children in whom we see many promising qualifications; though we live by good neighbors and are generally beloved where known; yet we ought not to take our rest in these things as our portion. . . . We ought to possess, enjoy and use them, with no other view but readily to quit them, whenever we are called to it, and to change them willingly and cheerfully for heaven.

At this point, we must bring imagination and reason together. In your mind's eye, imagine that you are walking along the road of life with this distinguished man at your side. Hear him speaking these words to you. (By the way, they are taken directly from the sermon noted above.)

- How does he challenge you?
- How does he encourage you?
- What will you take away from this encounter?

Here is what I gained from Edwards at this point. I found Edwards enormously encouraging as he affirms the goodness of God's creation. I can admire the world as I pass through it and pause to wonder at its great sights. Like the psalmist, I can be overwhelmed with some of the beauties and wonders of the creation. "The heavens declare the glory of the Lord!"

Yet I then pass on to another thought. If the creation is so wonderful, how much more so is its creator. And one day I will be with him! This thought fills me with anticipation, as I see the creation as a signpost pointing to its creator and intimating at least something of God's beauty and radiance. So, as Edwards rightly demands, I am ready to "change them willingly and cheerfully for heaven."

Edwards thus offers us a new perspective on our journey. As we travel, we are not being asked to ignore the beauties of the world through which we are passing. We may appreciate it and see it as a foretaste of the beauty of God, whom one day we shall see in all his radiance. Nor are we being asked to withdraw from the company and love of other people. Rather, we are asked to value and appreciate this, seeing it as an anticipation of being in the presence and love of God.

One day we shall have to relinquish what is good for what is the best. But in the meantime, we may begin to anticipate how wonderful that entry into the presence of God will be, and allow that thought to encourage and excite us as we travel on our journey.

⤳ WILDERNESS: DOUBT

The world is no friend to faith. When Israel left Egypt, it was propelled forward in its journey by enthusiasm and faith. Yet as time passed, faith faded, to be replaced by doubt. Some wanted to go back to Egypt. At least they had meat and bread back there. Somehow, the journey had become pointless. Israel faltered.

The problem of doubt is as real today as it was then. It remains a powerful challenge to the Christian life. Part of the problem is that many Christians want to know things for certain. We want to be like Thomas and be able to touch the risen Christ, to eat with him by the shore of Lake Tiberias. We want to be sure, fearing that the gospel is just too good to be true. We want there to be a pillar of cloud by day and a pillar of fire by night—something to prove the presence of God as we journey. It is so easy for us to identify with those words from the gospels: "Lord, I believe! Help my unbelief!" (Mark 9:24).

It is easy to see why doubt so readily gives way to despair. We feel the need to be sure—absolutely sure—about our faith. When others challenge us about the grounds of our faith, we would like to be able to point to sure proofs of the existence of God and the New Jerusalem that lies before us. We long to climb the mountain and see the Promised Land over the river. But we cannot. We walk by faith and not by sight. As the great hymn writer Isaac Watts (1674–1748) put it: "Do not expect to arrive at certainty in every subject which you pursue. There are a hundred things wherein we mortals . . . must be content with probability, where our best light and reasoning will reach no farther."

Doubt is our traveling companion in the wilderness, dogging our steps as we journey. It may withdraw from us for a season; its absence, however, proves temporary. Doubt is a lingering presence on the journey. We have to learn to cope with it.

Doubt is not simply an academic matter. It is not just that we cannot prove that God exists. It is an emotional issue in which we experience the terror of wondering whether there really is meaning in this vast universe; of whether there really is a God who loves us and values us; of whether we are simply part of a meaningless mechanical universe that neither knows nor cares that we exist. At moments like this, we need more than intellectual answers—we need to be enfolded in God's warm embrace and know his love and care.

Yet this is not a new or hitherto unknown experience on the journey of faith. Others who have made the journey before us have experienced the same bewilderment and distress. There is a bond of sympathy between ourselves and those who have gone before us, who have felt the pain of doubt as they struggled in their journey of faith. To read Psalm 42 is to enter into the world of someone who is distressed by his sense of the absence of God and his longing for the return of the sweet radiance of the Lord.

As the deer pants for streams of water
So my soul pants for you, O God.
My soul thirsts for God, for the living God.

As the Psalm progresses, it becomes clear why the writer feels so desolate. His God seems far away, and he is being taunted by those around him.

> My tears have been my food day and night
> While men say to me all day long, "Where is your God?"

Perhaps God has forgotten him? If so, he would be alone and lost. It is little wonder that he feels so downcast and disturbed.

Yet the psalmist is determined not to be discouraged. He puts into place a spiritual strategy for dealing with doubt—remembering and anticipating. He *remembers* how God was present in the past, and he *anticipates* the return of a sense of God's presence in the future. Seen from these perspectives, he can cope with his present distress.

First, he turns his mind to the past, when he knew the living reality of God:

> These things I remember as I pour out my soul
> How I used to go with the multitude,
> Leading the procession to the house of God
> With shouts of joy and thanksgiving.

All of us can cast our minds back to recall moments when we basked in the radiant presence of the Lord. In times of doubt, it is important to remember these—to write them down and recall how good they were. Israel knew the presence and power of the Lord as it left Egypt and in the bleaker times that followed constantly needed to be reminded of those days.

Yet the psalmist knows that the refreshing presence of God

will return. Even in his distress, he begins the luxurious process
of anticipating the renewal of fellowship with the Lord, savoring
its delights in advance:

> Put your hope in God
> For I will yet praise him.
> My Savior and my God.

God has *not* forgotten him; nor has God forgotten us. Our names
have been engraved on the palms of his hands (Isaiah 49:16).
There is no moment when his loving care for us falters, no point
at which he takes his eye off those whom he loves and for whom
his precious Son died.

It clearly helps to talk to someone who has experienced doubt
and learned how to cope with it. The time has come again to
hitch a ride along the road of faith with someone who has traveled it before us. . . .

Hitching a Ride: **Martin Luther**

Martin Luther (1483–1546) is one of the most important
Christian writers of the sixteenth century. He was at the fore-
front of the movement to reform and renew the Roman Catholic
church, which he regarded as having lost its way. Luther was
convinced that the church had lapsed into some kind of identity
crisis. It had become so heavily involved in the power politics and
high finance of the late Middle Ages that it had lost sight of its
true purpose. Luther saw his mission as being to recall the church
to rediscover the riches and joy of the gospel.

Although Luther began his career as a professor of biblical

studies at the University of Wittenberg, he soon expanded his influence beyond the somewhat narrow confines of academic life. One particular concern was the doctrine of justification by faith—that is, the question of what we need to do in order to be saved and enter into the presence of God. Luther felt—not without good reason—that the medieval church had become muddled in its thinking at this point and had allowed people to gain the impression that salvation could be purchased, or achieved through good works. The famous "indulgence controversy" centered on this important point. For Luther, salvation was the gracious gift of a gracious God, something that had to be accepted in trust and faith.

Luther placed considerable emphasis upon the total trustworthiness of God. The gospel could be trusted and believed because it rested on the promises of a God who could be relied upon. Luther was aware of how difficult many Christians found doubt and developed a number of ways of dealing with it. We shall explore two in this present section.

Both the approaches involve what is called the "theology of the cross"—that is, a way of thinking about God that focuses on the suffering and pain of Christ on the cross. Traditionally, this is an important way of recalling the costliness of our redemption. Reflecting on the pain and suffering of Christ as he died for us allows us to appreciate the incalculable wonders of God's graciousness and love in redeeming us. Luther takes this further and applies the image of the dying Christ to the issue of doubt.

To understand Luther's approach, you need to build a mental picture of Christ dying on the cross. Remember that meditation, in its proper Christian sense, means clearing your mind and allowing it to focus on an image from Scripture—in this case, the crucifixion. Try to set all intrusive thoughts about the world, family, friends, or whatever is troubling you to one side. Focus on Christ.

You might like to read one of the gospel accounts of the crucifixion, allowing the text to stimulate your imagination. Or you may find the following prompts helpful:

- Build up in your mind's eye the scene of the crucifixion. There is a small hill outside the walls of Jerusalem. There are three crosses. Focus on the middle one, and see Christ stretched out on it. He is there for you.
- Now fill in the fine detail. He is crowned with thorns, which are tearing at his skin. Blood is dribbling down. See his face, contorted with pain. Let your eyes move to his hands, nailed to the cross. The ugly wounds of the nails are slowly dripping with blood. It is a terrible sight, and you find it difficult to take in.
- Hear the crowds shouting out "Come down from the cross! Save yourself!" Yet he stays there and saved us instead. There is no limit to his love for us. He gave everything so that we might live.

Once you have built up this mental picture, ask why this is taking place. *He is doing this for us.* He didn't have to; he chose to. We matter so much to him. Anyone who suffers from low self-esteem needs to take this insight to heart. *You matter to the greatest one of all!* For Luther, meditating on the wounds of Christ was a superb antidote for any doubt we might have concerning the love of God for us. *He was wounded for us.* Each of those wounds is a token of the loving care of a compassionate God. Can you see how this

changes the way we think about ourselves? We are of such importance to him that he chose to undertake that suffering, pain, and
agony.

Form a mental picture of those wounds. Cherish them. It is by
them that we are healed. Each of them affirms the amazing love
of God for us. Each nail hammered into the body of the savior of
the world shouts out these words—"He loves us!" How can we
doubt someone who gave everything for us?

Luther also develops another approach to doubt, which focuses on the cross. Try to imagine that you are there on that first
Good Friday. Reenter the scene of the crucifixion. See yourself
among those watching Christ stumble along the painful and
lonely road to Calvary. Project yourself into the group of people
around the cross, watching Christ die. Yet as you do this, close
your mind to what happens next. You do not know about the
first Easter Day that lies so close to hand. When Jesus dies, you
think that is the end of the matter. Experience the cross as pure
cross; you do not know that the resurrection will transform everything.

Can you see why the disciples were distraught? We are told
that they were like sheep without a shepherd. Sure, they should
have known there was to be a resurrection. But that seemed to
have been forgotten in the face of the grim and harsh reality of
the death of Christ on the cross of shame and dereliction. The
person on whom all their hopes were founded had been destroyed—and, it seemed, their hopes had died with him. Try to
enter into the experience of those disciples. Don't just understand—go deeper. Try to project yourself into their shattered
worlds.

Take a moment to focus on the words that follow. Dwell on

them, absorbing their emotional impact. What kind of experience do they describe? What is it like to know them, not just as words in a dictionary, but as real life experiences?

- Despair
- Hopelessness
- Bewilderment

We shall never fully understand the joy of Easter unless we experience the despair of that first Good Friday.

Now we can understand Luther's point. Life on the road of faith bears an uncomfortable likeness to that first Good Friday. We experience our hopes being dashed, our firm beliefs being questioned, and our experiential world thrown into turmoil by what we meet and see. Like those first disciples after the death of Christ, there are times when we find ourselves bewildered and don't know where to turn.

Yet those fears and that despair were transformed on the first Easter Day. The first statement of the good news was simply that Christ was risen—that the one who had died had been raised again. As the astonishing implications of this staggering development began to saturate the minds of the disciples, their outlook on life was transfigured. Despair gave way to joy, a joy that was heightened precisely because of the despair that preceded it. Good Friday was seen in a new light. What seemed pointless, hopeless, and bewildering could be seen in a new and awe-inspiring light: it was the majestic means of achieving perhaps the greatest miracle of all—the redemption of humanity.

Luther challenges and encourages us to take this framework and apply it to our experience as we journey through the wilderness. As on the first Good Friday, we will encounter despair, perplexity, and a sense of hopelessness. Yet we need to see these as we now see that first Good Friday—from the perspective of Easter Day. The cross is to be seen from the standpoint of the resurrection. The Christian faith affirms that at present we see things only darkly, as in mirror or through distorting glass (1 Corinthians 13:12); but one day, we will see God face-to-face, and will finally see the big picture, which makes sense of what went before.

So how does Luther challenge and encourage us? What can we take away from the time we have spent with him, listening to his insights? There can be no doubt that Luther's main aim is to reassure us. We must trust in God's promises and not in our perceptions. Luther challenges us to take courage and keep walking in faith. We may not have answers to all the questions, but we trust in a loving, caring, and totally trustworthy God, the "God of all comfort, who comforts us in all troubles" (2 Corinthians 1:4).

And with that thought, we press on through the wilderness, knowing that each step we take brings us nearer to the Promised Land.

❧ OASIS: REFRESHMENT

Anyone who has struggled through a dry and rocky wilderness needs rest and refreshment. Just as a parched land cries out for rain, so we long to be cooled and revitalized by drafts of fresh water. It was natural for the prophets to see the coming of rain to a dry land as a powerful analogy of the human need to be restored and renewed.

Travelers through the desert wastes were kept going by the thought of an oasis—the luxury of a pool of water, in the blissful shade of date palms, around which weary travelers could find rest and peace. Soon they would have to move on again. But in the meantime, they experienced the sweet calm of freedom from toil and exertion. It was a rare and refreshing moment of delight.

Psalm 63 brings out the yearning for spiritual refreshment after an exhausting struggle along the road of faith:

> O God, you are my God
> Earnestly I seek you
> My soul thirsts for you
> My body longs for you
> In a dry and weary land
> Where there is no water.

The psalm vividly depicts the weariness of an arduous journey through the desert. It generates a mental image of the journey that allows us to enter the experiential world of a tired and weary traveler who longs for rest and refreshment. But where is it to be found?

The psalm makes the point that it is God alone who can refresh and renew us along the journey of faith. Just as the exertions of physical travel cause us to hunger and thirst for food and drink, the journey of faith must be sustained by the living God.

Paul makes the point that Israel was sustained in this way

during its wilderness wanderings. The people of Israel "ate the same spiritual food and drank the same spiritual drink; for they drank from the spiritual rock that accompanied them, and that rock was Christ" (I Corinthians 10:3–4). We can develop this idea of being nourished on the road of faith by meditating on two New Testament themes that emphasize the need to be sustained by Christ throughout that journey. Both these themes are found in John's gospel; taken together, they provide a rich and reassuring insight into our journey.

First, Jesus speaks of giving us water, which becomes "a spring of water welling up to eternal life" (John 4:14). Dwell on this image and begin to appreciate it. The point being made is that ordinary water satisfies temporarily; the water that Jesus brings brings permanent refreshment. Second, Jesus speaks of being the "bread of life" (John 6:51). Unlike the manna given to Israel in the wilderness, anyone who eats this bread will be satisfied fully and will live forever. Ordinary bread leads to death; this bread leads to eternal life.

It is helpful to pause and meditate on these two images. Both speak of refreshment; both declare that this refreshment is to be only in Christ. Jesus does not tell his audience that he will show them the bread of life or that he will take them to some special place where it may be found. No; he himself is that bread. To feed on Christ is to be sustained and nourished along the road of faith. So how are we to make sense of this? What does it mean to "feed on Christ"? One answer was given by the great English Baptist preacher, Charles Haddon Spurgeon (1834–92).

In a celebrated sermon preached on the first Sunday of 1855, Spurgeon spoke movingly of our need for refreshment along the road of faith and unhesitatingly identified where that refreshment was to be found—in the contemplation of Christ.

There is, in contemplating Christ, a balm for every wound; in musing on the Father, there is a quietus for every grief; and in the influence of the Holy Ghost, there is a balsam for every sore. Would you lose your sorrow? Would you drown your cares? Then go, plunge yourself in the Godhead's deepest sea; be lost in his immensity; and you shall come forth as from a couch of rest, refreshed and invigorated. I know nothing which can so comfort the soul; so speak peace to the winds of trial, as a devout musing upon the subject of the Godhead.

These were bold and powerful words, made all the more remarkable because the preacher was a mere twenty years old at the time. Spurgeon was expressing a wisdom beyond his years, drawing on the distilled insights of travelers along this road before him. Rather than worry about how someone so young could express such profound ideas, let us see how we can make use of them.

For Spurgeon, meditating on Christ is profoundly consoling. Notice how he uses a series of images to explore the impact of meditating upon Christ for the tired soul. Notice how images relating to tiredness, stress, and wounds are scattered throughout this brief passage. Those undertaking the journey are expected to be battered, bruised, and weary. Spurgeon urges his hearers to plunge themselves into the immensity of God and emerge from this refreshed, healed, and consoled.

One way of doing this is through worship and adoration.

Worship is the human response to catching a glimpse of God in all his radiance and glory. It is a moment in which words fail us and we fall to our knees in joy, wonder, and amazement. We realize that human language is simply not capable of doing justice to the majesty and glory of the Lord. Worship refreshes us precisely because it forces us to raise our eyes upward and appreciate the immensity and grandeur of our maker and redeemer. And excited and invigorated by this vision, we return to the Christian life with a new sense of commitment and renewed energy.

Perhaps something like this happened to the prophet Isaiah. We learn that the prophet had a vision of the Lord in the temple, a vision in which the glory of the Lord shone forth, overwhelming Isaiah. In the light of this revelation of the glorious radiance of God, Isaiah fell to his knees, knowing that he was a sinner who should never have been allowed to behold something so wonderful. Yet as we read on, we find that the vision of the Lord has energized him. When he hears the Lord asking who will serve him, the voice that replies is his own: "Here I am! Send me!" A vision of the wondrous glory of God propels us into his willing service.

Can we catch a glimpse of that glory? Perhaps we shall have to wait until we enter through the gates of the New Jerusalem before we see the Lord in all his glory. Yet every now and then, we catch something of a glimpse of that glory—and it is enough to keep us going on the long journey to the heavenly city. We need to pray for a constant renewal of our vision of the Lord as we travel.

But there is another way of being refreshed along the journey, in the manner suggested by Spurgeon. This is to be found in the writings of one of the most important evangelical thinkers of the twentieth century. And so we prepare to hitch a ride with this man, in order that we can rest and learn.

Hitching a Ride: J. I. Packer

James Innell Packer was born in the English cathedral city of Gloucester in 1927. He studied classics at school and then went to Oxford University in 1944 to continue his studies. He became a Christian during his first term at Oxford. Shortly afterward, he began to develop an interest in the writings of great Puritan theologians such as John Owen and Richard Baxter. He found that they were far more realistic about the problems of the Christian life than many of those who came to speak at Christian Union meetings.

Packer was academically able. After completing his studies in classics at Oxford, he went on to gain First Class Honours in theology. His interest in the Puritan writers led to him undertaking doctoral work at Oxford on some aspects of the religious thought of Richard Baxter. Yet Packer would find his calling not so much as an academic theologian but as one with a rare and important gift for making theology and spirituality more accessible to a wide readership.

Packer first became aware of his gift for explanation during a year spent teaching at a college in North London. He would later apply it during several periods spent in theological education in England and especially during his long period as professor of theology at Regent College, Vancouver (1979–97). One of

Packer's best-known works is *Knowing God* (1973). This work can be seen as standing in the great tradition of Puritan spirituality so much admired by Spurgeon. One of its most important themes is the need to know God fully not simply to know things *about* God.

It is a wonderful thing that we have the privilege of knowing God. Yet there is something even more astonishing that we must grasp and treasure—*that God knows us.* Even before we were born, God knew us. He knew that some of us would fail him on account of our weakness and others through our rebelliousness. He knew that others would love him from the moment they were capable of loving anything. Yet in all things, this God loves and sustains us. God already knows us, exactly as we are. There is no pretense or deceit; he sees us as we are, penetrating the facades we erect to preserve our public image.

God knows us (Psalm 139:1). Imagine being known, warts and all (to use Oliver Cromwell's famous phrase). For some, this is a deeply threatening idea. Yet, to others, including myself, this is a deeply reassuring thought. When we pray, we don't need to pretend about anything. We don't need to live in some make-believe world in which we constantly struggle to live up to the image we have created for ourselves. In prayer, we enter into the caring presence of one who created us and knows us through and through. We come as we are, asking God to make us what he would have us be, entrusting ourselves to the one who can heal and renew us.

So often we feel we need to know more about God, when in reality we need to know God more intimately. As we saw, Spurgeon asked his hearers to plunge themselves "in the God-head's deepest sea; be lost in his immensity; and you shall come forth as from a couch of rest, refreshed and invigorated." Packer, like Spurgeon, asks us to go deeper. He draws an important distinction between "knowing by description" and "knowing by acquaintance." He affirms the importance of what he terms "relational knowledge," by which he understands "knowledge that comes to us in the relation of commitment and trust, faith and reliance."

In *Knowing God*, Packer brings out how our relationship with God involves our mind, will, and emotions. We need to work on each of these. It is so easy to become spiritually impoverished by neglecting vital aspects of our relationship with God. Knowing more about God may feed the mind; although it will certainly protect us from error and confusion, it will probably not nourish us anywhere else. We need to dedicate ourselves purposefully to loving and serving God more—in other words, to direct our wills toward God with a new intensity and commitment. And we also need to allow our feelings to be involved in this. As Packer writes:

> *Knowing God is a matter of* personal involvement, *in mind, will and feeling. It would not, indeed, be a fully personal relationship otherwise. To get to know another person, you have to commit yourself to his company and interests, and be ready to identify with his concerns. Without this, your relationship with him can only be superficial and flavorless.*

Packer illustrates this point by considering two people who are in love, who spend time with each other and come to know each other's longings.

> *As they thus open their hearts to each other by what they say and do, each "tastes" the quality of the other, for sorrow or for joy. They have identified themselves with, and so are personally and emotionally involved in, each other's concerns. They feel for each other, as well as thinking of each other. This is an essential aspect of the knowledge which friends have of each other; and the same applies to the Christian's knowledge of God which, as we have seen, is itself a relationship of friends.*

Spiritual refreshment is thus acquired by spending time with God, by deepening our commitment to him, and by identifying ourselves with what we know matters to him. It involves our mind, will, and feelings. Knowing God thus has an *emotional* dimension—an aspect of the relationship we so easily play down on account of our fear of being thought to be "self-absorbed" or irrational.

> *We must not lose sight of the fact that knowing God is an emotional relationship, as well as an intellectual and volitional one, and could not indeed be a deep relationship between persons were it not so. The believer is and must be emotionally involved in the victories and vicissitudes of God's cause in the world. . . . The believer rejoices when his God is honored and feels the acutest distress when he sees God flouted. . . . The Christian feels shame and grief when convicted of having failed his Lord (see, for instance, Psalm 51 and Luke 22:61–2), and from time to time knows transports of delight as God brings home to him in one way or another the glory of the everlasting love with which he has been loved.*

Packer's words pose a powerful challenge to the cold rationalism that has been the scourge of sections of Western Christianity for the last two centuries.

So what insights does our traveling companion offer us? How will what he has shared with us refresh us as we prepare for the next stage of our journey? As we huddle around the campfire under the leaves of the oasis palm trees, what counsel does he offer to prepare us to head off into the bleak desert again tomorrow?

Perhaps the most powerful insight Packer offers us is also his simplest. We must learn to know our traveling companion better as we travel along the road of faith. For we are not alone on the road. It is not merely others who have found the living God who accompany us; it is the living God himself. His presence guards, consoles, and challenges us, energizing us as we journey. The God who is the goal of our traveling is also our companion on that journey.

Packer asks that we come to know this God better. We must trust in him and commit ourselves to him. He cares for us and will guide us along the way. We need to know that care, not simply as a theological opinion but as a life-giving and life-sustaining reality upon which the journey of faith depends from its beginning to its end.

What matters supremely, therefore, is not, in the last analysis, the fact that I know God, but the larger fact which underlies it—the fact that he knows *me. I am graven on the palms of his hands. I am never out of his mind. All my knowledge of him depends on his sustained initiative in knowing me. I know him, because he first knew me, and continues to know me. He knows me as a friend, one who loves me; and there is no moment when his eye is off me, or his attention distracted from me, and no moment, therefore, when his care falters.*

Those words are enormously encouraging. They summarize in an admirably compact manner a central biblical theme—the continual care of God for those he loves. Read Packer's words again; then read Psalm 121, which follows. But read it slowly.

I lift my eyes to the hills—
Where does my help come from?
My help comes from the Lord,
The Maker of heaven and earth.
He will not let your foot slip—
He who watches over you will not slumber.
Indeed, he who watches over Israel
Will neither slumber nor sleep.
The Lord watches over you—
The Lord is your shade at your right hand.
The sun will not harm you by day
Nor the moon by night.
The Lord will keep you from all harm—
He will watch over your life;
The Lord will watch over your coming and going
Both now and forevermore.

Can you see how comforting those words would be to someone setting out on a journey? The journeyer would be anxious about the dangers and hardships he would have to endure, such as climbing steep and rugged hills or coping with a harsh climate. Yet the psalm reaffirms the constant, continual care of God throughout that journey. Packer would want us to grasp that *we who know God are in turn known by God*—and that his loving care embraces and enfolds us wherever our journey of faith takes us.

So, in the knowledge of that care and constant presence, we prepare to set out on the second stage of our journey.

Chapter 5

The Second Stage

As Israel traveled through the wilderness, tiredness and sheer rebelliousness began to set in. Why are we doing this? Where is this Promised Land? The lure of milk and honey was strong. Yet it proved difficult for the people of Israel to hold on to that vision when they saw nothing but the arid and bleak desert landscape around them.

There seems to be a road that leads remorselessly from weariness to rebellion. In the barren wastes of the wilderness, we are confronted with the grim and harsh realities of our own weaknesses and failings. We come to know ourselves as never before. For many Christians, the wilderness is a place of isolation in which we have the opportunity to identify and confront the hidden sins and fears that threaten to destroy us as people and prevent us from reaching our journey's end.

The wilderness can thus be a place of purification, somewhere we can examine ourselves, face up to our failings, and put things right. It is a place of exile, not a permanent home. It is not where we are meant to be. Yet our wanderings in that place of exile can prepare us for that homecoming, not least in that it gives us a new awareness of how much we long to return home. We therefore turn to consider how we can regard this world as a place of exile. . . .

⚜ LANDMARK: EXILE

What are we doing in this world? Are we *meant* to be here? These questions are rightly asked by those journeying through life. So what landmark can we identify that helps us get our bearings in this respect? We have already seen the importance of one landmark—creation. What others can be identified?

The Christian journey can be thought of in terms of a framework of four landmarks:

- ⚜ Creation
- ⚜ Exile
- ⚜ Redemption
- ⚜ Consummation

The landmark of exile affirms that we have been expelled from Eden. We no longer live in paradise, although it is our passionate hope to return there in the future. On account of sin, we are exiled from our true home and destiny. As John Stott remarks, every Christian is "a citizen of heaven, and an alien and exile on earth, a pilgrim traveling to the celestial city."

To speak of life in this world as an "exile" suggests two

important themes, each of which helps us to make some sense of our situation.

1. "Exile" means that we are not living in our homeland. This world is not our home; our true destiny lies elsewhere.
2. One of the most powerful forces to animate the life of those in exile is the thought of finally returning home. This hope gives a sense of purpose to life.

So what is this landmark all about? To gain a full appreciation of the importance of this marker on the road of faith, we need to consider how the theme of "exile" is developed in the Old and New Testaments. Perhaps one of the most traumatic events to have taken place in the history of the people of God was the capture of the city of Jerusalem by invading Babylonian armies in 586 B.C. The defenses and main buildings of the city were destroyed and many of its people deported to captivity in Babylon. The period of exile had begun; it would not end until the defeat of the Babylonian armies under the Persians in 539 B.C.

The exile thus lasted for more than a generation. Many of those who had been deported did not live long enough to return home. Many were born in captivity in Babylon and knew "Jerusalem" only as a memory spoken of in hushed tones by their parents. The return to their homeland of Jerusalem was something they longed for but never expected to see. It is impossible to read Psalm 137 without experiencing a sense of immense sadness and distress:

By the rivers of Babylon we sat and wept
When we remembered Zion

There on the poplars we hung our harps
For there our captors asked us for sons
Our tormentors demanded songs of joy;
They said: "Sing to us one of the songs of Zion!"
How can we sing the songs of Zion while in a foreign
    land?

The great Old Testament prophets saw this period of exile in two ways. First, it was seen as a *judgment* on Israel. The people of God had wandered away from their God and had forgotten him. They had lapsed into all kinds of pagan ways. Exile was the direct result of their sin. Just as Adam and Eve were expelled from Eden through sin, so the people of God were driven out of their beloved Jerusalem. Second, it was seen as providing an opportunity for *repentance and renewal.* The enforced period of exile would be a period of self-examination, confession, and refreshment, which offered God's people the chance to rediscover and reclaim their distinct identity as the people of God.

The period of exile was thus an opportunity for reflection and regaining identity and perspective. We need to appreciate how significant this theme can be for our own personal journey of faith. To do this, we need to do more than *understand* the concept of "exile"; we need to *experience* the emotional turmoil it creates. This challenges us to enter into Israel's experience of exile and discover its impact upon both our minds and feelings. So let us conduct a thought experiment and see how it helps us understand the journey.

Imagine, as a Jew, that you have lived in the city of Jerusalem all your life. Like the psalmist (see Psalm 87), you take enormous delight in its buildings and its history. The temple of the Lord is one of the architectural wonders of the region. The city walls are impregnable and a source of great pride to the inhabitants of Jerusalem. The great kings David and Solomon ruled there. The future messiah will be born within its walls. Try to imagine the sense of privilege you would feel at living in such a city.

Then a foreign army arrives and lays siege to the city. Everyone hopes and prays that they will go away. But they stay. Finally, they breach the defenses of the city and pour in. They ransack the city, destroying the temple and the city walls. Imagine the sense of anger, despair, and utter devastation you would experience as you see this happening in front of your eyes. Rebuilding what has been destroyed will be the work of a lifetime.

Yet there is worse to come. The invaders round up most of the population and begin marching you eastward. Slowly, the ruins of Jerusalem recede into the distance. Finally, they pass out of sight. You realize that you may never see the homeland again. Can you generate within yourself the emotions that would have been felt by the people of Jerusalem as they left their native land behind? And their longing to return home when they were forced to live in Babylon?

We can gain something of a sense of their despair, demoralization, and longings from reading the literature of the period. Two themes can be identified, each of which illuminates our situation:

- Looking backward, with a sense of nostalgia mingled with despair. The people of Jerusalem recall their beloved city, longing to be there, and reliving the memories of the past.

* Looking forward, in the hope that they will one day return to their homeland and rebuild the ruined city of
Jerusalem.

We see here the distinctive pattern we noted earlier (p. 24),
remembering and anticipating. This helps illuminate our own situation
by offering us a framework to illuminate our own situation.

* *We are in exile.*
* *We live in the hope of returning home.*

For many Christian writers, such as Augustine or C. S. Lewis, we
experience a sense of longing that is really a memory of the
past—a longing to return to Eden.

Paul develops this theme of absence from the homeland in his
letter to the Philippians. He affirms to his readers that (Philippians 3:20) "our citizenship is in heaven. And we eagerly await a
Savior from there, the Lord Jesus Christ." Paul's imagery is immensely evocative and would have been readily understood and
appreciated by his readers in Philippi. Why? Because at the time
of Paul's letter, Philippi was a Roman colony. Its strategic location in Macedonia made it an important military center, and
large numbers of Roman soldiers passed through the city. In
addition, there was a large Roman civilian population. Philippi
was proud of its ties with Rome, including its language (Latin
seems to have been more widely spoken than Greek) and laws.
Roman institutions served as the model in many areas of its
communal life.

Paul uses the image of the church as a "colony of heaven" to bring out several leading aspects of Christian existence. By speaking of the Christian community in this way, he naturally encourages his readers to think of the Christian church as an outpost of heaven in a foreign land. It speaks the language of that homeland and is governed by its laws—despite the fact that the world around it speaks a different language and obeys a different set of laws. Its institutions are based on those of its homeland. And, one day, its citizens will return to that homeland to take up all the privileges and rights that that citizenship confers. The Christian's citizenship is in heaven, and it is to this homeland that we will one day return.

This image thus lends dignity and new depths of meaning to the Christian life, especially the tension between the "now" and "not yet," and the bittersweet feeling of being outsiders to a culture in the world and yet not of the world. The Romans at Philippi could be said to be "in" Macedonia and yet not "of" Macedonia in that they knew that they were Romans who would one day go back to their homeland. They may have lived in Philippi; their hearts were firmly attached to Rome.

We can therefore think of ourselves as exiles in this world. As Adam and Eve were evicted from Eden through sin, so are we cut off from our homeland. But the hope of return is there. As Paul reminded the Christians at Philippi, our citizenship is in heaven—and we eagerly await the savior who will bring us home, so that we may rejoice to be where we belong. Our journey will lead us to our homeland, where we shall finally have rest.

The time has now come to hitch a ride with someone who has wrestled with the issues of being sojourners in the world and exiles from our homeland. . . .

Hitching a Ride: *Anselm of Canterbury*

The Middle Ages witnessed a remarkable growth in writings on Christian spirituality. One of the most important writers of this period is Anselm of Canterbury (c. 1033–1109). Anselm was born in Aosta in the northern Italian region of Lombardy but eventually settled in France. In 1059 he entered the monastery of Bec in Normandy, where he became prior in 1063 and abbot in 1078. In 1093, Anselm became Archbishop of Canterbury. William I of Normandy had invaded England in 1066 and was busy appointing Normans to senior positions in the English church and state.

Anselm disliked the responsibilities that accompanied this position and is remembered chiefly for his writings, of which two may be singled out for particular mention. The *Monologion* (1078) is an extended meditation upon God, which includes what has come to be known as the ontological argument for the existence of God. The treatise *Cur Deus homo* ("Why God Became Man," 1098) set out a highly influential account of the death of Christ and the necessity of the incarnation. Yet Anselm was also much in demand as a spiritual adviser, and many of his prayers and letters of spiritual guidance have survived. They are noted for their strongly reflective character and the way in which they draw their readers into meditation on the Christian faith.

In his "Prayer to Christ," Anselm explores the theme of longing to see God when exile on this earth is ended. Anselm remarked that the prayer was intended to "stir up the mind of the reader to the love of God," and urged that it was "not to be read in a turmoil, but quietly; not skimmed or hurried through, but taken a little at a time, with deep and thoughtful meditation." So read what follows slowly, absorbing the imagery, and noting how Anselm engages both the reason and the emotions. The prayer is directly addressed to God:

> I thirst for you, I hunger for you, I desire you,
> I sigh for you, I covet you:
> I am like an orphan deprived of the presence of a very kind
>   father,
> who, weeping and wailing, does not cease to cling to
> the dear face with his whole heart. . . .
> All this I hold with unwavering faith,
> and weep over the hardship of exile,
> hoping in the sole consolation of your coming,
> ardently longing for the glorious contemplation of your
>   face.

The prayer opens with a passionate declaration of the longing of the soul for God. Note how each of the verbs in the first sentence expresses a longing or emptiness. The cumulative effect of this imagery of yearning is to bring home how empty and unfulfilled we are without the comforting presence of God. Realizing how much we long for God makes us want to be in his presence and be able to bask and delight in the radiance of his face.

This sense of longing for God is now supplemented with two images of separation—those of "orphan" and "exile." Each of these images demands to have its *rational content understood* and its *emotional implications experienced.*

The image of the "orphan" invites us to consider the plight of a child who has been "deprived of the presence of a very kind father." What was once a familiar, loving, and caring presence has become a painful absence. The child longs to see her father again and lives in hope of doing so. Yet at present she knows little other than sorrow and grief, mourning the loss of his kindly face. She lives suspended in the emotional chasm between the memory of the past and the hope of the future.

Similar themes are associated with the "hardship of exile." Anselm explores the pain of separation, pointing out the sense of longing for God. As Augustine of Hippo once put it in a well-known prayer to God: "You have made us for yourself, and our hearts are restless until they find their rest in you." Only coming into the presence of God and being able to contemplate his wonderful face will ease this pain and grief. Yet Anselm does not allow himself to wallow in self-pity. His longing for God is the result of exile from the homeland; one day, that exile will be ended, and he will be in the presence of God. His experience of longing for God is thus interpreted in three different yet clearly related ways:

1. Our present situation is that of being orphaned or being in exile—that is, separated and cut off from a full knowledge of God. We sense the pain of separation.

2. The realization that we are in exile helps us to appreciate that we are in the world but not of the world. The world is not our homeland; it is our place of exile, and we must look beyond it, while nevertheless appreciating whatever beauty it may possess and attempting to make it a better place. We are sojourners in this land, not permanent residents.

3. This realization encourages us to look forward with eager

anticipation to finally being in the radiant and glorious presence of God, and beholding his face.

Anselm helps us to understand our situation better so that we can journey onward in hope. We shall never find the joy and wonder that we seek en route, even if we experience welcome anticipations of them along the road. Yet we are reassured of what awaits us at journey's end, and encouraged to long for this even more.

So, encouraged by the insights of our fellow traveler Anselm, we prepare to enter the wilderness once more.

✤ WILDERNESS: FAILURE

So many of us are impatient with our faith. The journey we are invited to undertake is a long haul and delivers its benefits in the longer term. We have got to learn the hardest of all lessons—that we need to be patient. God seems to operate on a time scale that takes no account of our personal agendas and deadlines. The reality of life is such that we have to adapt ourselves to God's way of doing things rather than expect him to adapt to ours.

To make this point, Jesus told the story of the seed growing in secret (Mark 4:26–29). The seed, once sown, disappears from view. Even though it is germinating and growing beneath the earth, we cannot see this from our limited vantage point above. Only when the growing shoot finally breaks through the soil and announces its presence to the world can we really grasp the fact that, up to that point, it has been growing in secret.

Similarly, we have to face up to the fact that the seed of the gospel takes a long time to break through in our lives. There will be long periods of invisibility, silence, and darkness in our spiritual growth. We have just got to get used to this and realize that it does not imply any weakness or failure on the part of God, or lack of commitment or care on his part. It was Thomas Aquinas who pointed out, back in the thirteenth century, that the apparently leisurely way God deals with us does not reflect any failing on his part but the weak and fallen human nature with which he has to deal.

The long journey of the people of Israel from Egypt to Canaan was characterized by failure as much as by success. Alongside the great triumphs—such as the crossing of the Red Sea and the entry into the Promised Land—there were failures. Sometimes those were failures to trust God; at other times, they were personal failings that threatened to divide, demoralize, or destroy the people of God. It is important to avoid romanticizing the wandering of Israel in the wilderness as if this was a period of nothing but faith and obedience. As the biblical accounts indicate, Israel's behavior left much to be desired, and we must be thoroughly realistic about its weaknesses and failings. Why?

Because we show precisely those same weaknesses and failings.

Few things discourage us more than failure. Indeed, failure is one of the most fundamental of all wilderness experiences. It can have devastating effects. Those who fail often feel that they are useless and have no place in God's purposes. They are tempted to sit down by the side of the road and travel no farther. For them, the journey has ended. What point is there in going on?

The people of God have been there before—and have triumphed over both their failure and their reaction to it. The supreme example is Peter, and we must give the most careful attention to his story.

The scene takes place as Jesus and his disciples are walking to the Mount of Olives. The last supper has ended, and Jesus is preparing his disciples for what must happen next—his betrayal, arrest, and crucifixion. He also warns them that they will fall away. They will not be able to cope with the pressure (Mark 14:27–31). Peter is indignant. He is absolutely convinced that he would *never* abandon or betray Jesus. Jesus knows otherwise; Peter, he declares, will deny him three times that very night.

It is easy to criticize Peter. Yet we need to enter into his world and realize that he was convinced that he could cope with the pressure. He could not have known how tough things were going to get. We read the account of Peter's denial with sadness mingled with reproach (Mark 14:66–72). After Peter had denied Jesus three times, he realized what had happened—and broke down in tears. What greater failure could there be?

Peter had, quite simply, failed Jesus. He had let him down utterly. What hope could there be for him in the light of this spectacular failure? Surely Peter could have no further place in God's purposes?

Perhaps those are natural conclusions to draw. But they fail to take account of the power and graciousness of God. As we all know, Peter recovered from this failure and went on to lead the apostles into a period of major expansion of the Christian faith. In John's gospel, we learn that Jesus spoke to Peter privately (John 21:15–19), asking him the same question three times: "Do you truly love me?" Peter answers in the affirmative each time, with increasing vehemence. With each of these three responses, he set behind him each of his earlier denials of Jesus. Peter is thought to have been martyred at Rome around 64. He would not deny Jesus again.

We can all learn from this example—and take hope from it. Perhaps we fail because we are unrealistic and naive. Perhaps we fail to realize how tough things can get. Yet we are dealing with a gracious and forgiving God who knows our weaknesses. When we fail—as, sadly, we will—we need to allow God to put us back on our feet again and recommission us in his service. God has a long history of taking self-confessed failures and doing great things through them. Perhaps when we fail, we are most receptive to the grace of God.

Paul had to learn that lesson the hard way. He tells us that God chose to humble him through a "thorn in the flesh" (2 Corinthians 12:1–10)—perhaps an illness that prevented him from carrying out some of the missionary undertakings he had planned. He needed to be taught not to trust in his own strength but to rely on God. In his weakness, he heard God speak these words: "My grace is sufficient for you, for my power is made perfect in weakness." Failure discloses our weakness and helps us discover God's power.

At this point, we should allow another voice to join in our conversation and illuminate it with his wisdom. And so we turn to welcome a traveling companion, who joins us on the road and shares his hard-won wisdom with us.

Hitching a Ride: *Alexander MacLaren*

Alexander MacLaren (1826–1910) was one of the greatest Scottish preachers of the nineteenth century, even if his ministry

took place virtually entirely in England. Born in Glasgow, Mac-
Laren began his ministry in the south of England in 1845. He
served as pastor of Portland Chapel, a somewhat dilapidated
building in the port of Southampton, for over twelve years. Although his career began in obscurity, it was not long before word
of his preaching began to spread. In 1858, he was called to
pastor the large and prestigious Union Chapel in the great northern industrial city of Manchester. He remained in that position
for more than forty years, preaching his final sermon in June
1903.

MacLaren saw his ministry as focusing virtually entirely on
preaching and drew large crowds throughout his Manchester period. Initially, he had no intention of publishing his sermons,
although he prepared detailed outlines of them all. However, a
member of his congregation jotted down his first series of Manchester sermons in shorthand and arranged for them to be published. They proved to be highly popular. After his retirement in
1903, MacLaren was able to expand his sermon notes to produce
a series of thirty-two volumes of expository sermons.

One of the finest such sermons is based on John 16:33: "Be
of good cheer; I have overcome the world." MacLaren saw this
passage as having momentous implications for those who were
conscious of failure. Indeed, he even entitled the resulting sermon "Victory in Failure." Failure, for MacLaren, is a potential
point for growth. So often we trust in our own strength and
need to learn to rely on the strength that God provides. So
often we regard as successes those who are in reality failures.
Those who seem to have conquered the world have, in reality,
been conquered by it. MacLaren makes this point through a
well-known analogy.

Do you remember the old story about the soldier that shouted out that he had caught a prisoner? And the officer said: "Bring him along." And the soldier answered: "But he won't come." "Then come yourself." And the answer was: "He won't let me." That is the kind of victory that many of our successful people have got; these are so hampered and held in its chains that early noble visions have passed away, and are smiled at now.

Failure is so often defined with reference to the standards of the world; there is a need to realize that what the world counts as failure may count as a crown in the sight of God. We are being asked to see what we think of as "successes" and "failures" from God's perspective, not ours.

The classic example of this is the cross of Christ. The world regarded Christ's death on the cross as a failure; in reality, it was a victory over the world. MacLaren insists that we learn from this seminal insight and take courage. "The way to overcome our troubles is to bear them; the way to conquer our crosses is willingly to lay them on our shoulders." Christ has overcome the world; we share in that victory.

Look again at my text, at its immediate context, and notice, just before, our Lord has said this: "In the world you shall have tribulation; in Me you shall have peace." Very well; there are two spheres, if I may so say, in both of which the Christian dwells—in the world and in Christ— the one full of afflictions and trials and temptations; the other like some sequestered dale in the midst of an island in the raging sea, where the wind never blows, and all is peace. In Christ, peace; in the world, tribulation.

Those who experience the pain and grief of failure are encouraged to look to the cross and find comfort and consolation in Christ:

> *Put your trust in Him as the sacrifice for your sins, and as the spirit of your lives you look to Him not only as example, not only as pattern, but as power; you think of Him, not only as dying on the cross for you, but as living in you, and then you will find, as sure as He lives, you will find that He has conquered, and that His conquest is for you. . . . So be of good cheer; you will have to fight, thank God for it; you will have to fight; you will be beaten as sure as you live if you try to master the world without Jesus; but if you will lay your hands by faith on the Lamb of God, and if you will open your hearts and lives to the influences of His triumphant Spirit, then He will give you a share in His conflict, His conquest, and His royal repose.*

So how does MacLaren encourage and challenge us? He challenges us to admit that our thinking on failure has been shaped by the standards of the world, not the values and themes of the gospel. Our attitudes to failure show that we have been taken captive by the spirit of the age, when we should have yielded to the Spirit of Christ. Perhaps his greatest challenge to us is to demand that we reconsider how we view failure. Failure is so easily seen in worldly terms, as something purely negative. For MacLaren, it is the key to spiritual growth. Yesterday's failure is today's opportunity for growth, which leads to tomorrow's success. It reminds us of our need to recognize our weakness and to realize our need to trust in God—not ourselves!

As we struggle along the road of faith, we will encounter failure—sometimes our own failures, sometimes the failures of others. We need to confront them; yet we need also to learn from them. We must keep learning as we travel—learning more about the God who so loves us and also about ourselves. John Calvin reminds us that true wisdom consists of knowing God and knowing ourselves. As we travel, we come to learn more about ourselves. We discover strengths and weaknesses we had not known before. MacLaren asks us to identify these weaknesses and ensure that they become points of growth and grounds for hope.

MacLaren thus encourages us to trust in the promises of Christ and to realize that by faith we share in a victory the world regarded as a defeat. His sermon ended with the following stirring words—may they encourage us as we struggle through the wilderness. "To him that overcomes will I grant to sit with Me on My throne, even as I overcame, and am sat down with My Father on His throne."

And encouraged by this reminder of our final goal, we prepare to press onward. . . .

OASIS: REST

Weary travelers need rest. After a long and tiring journey across a barren and inhospitable landscape, everyone needs to relax and unwind. The tiredness that is so important a feature of life on the road of faith is something that we must acknowledge, along with our own inability to cope with it. Yet in his grace and love, God is able to renew us and enable us to continue the journey in hope.

We find these themes of human tiredness and divine renewal in one of the great prophetic visions of the Old Testament (Isaiah 40:39–41). The prophet foresees the people of Jerusalem returning home from exile in Babylon and the exhaustion they will experience. Yet alongside that exhaustion, he sees the gentle and refreshing hand of God at work.

> [The Lord] gives strength to the weary
> and increases the power of the weak.
> Even youths grow tired and weary,
> And young men stumble and fall;
> But those who hope in the Lord will renew their strength.
> They will soar on wings like eagles;
> They will run and not grow weary,
> They will walk, and not be faint.

This great vision of the divine renewal of those who wait on the Lord is enormously comforting and reassuring.

Yet many of us feel guilty resting or relaxing. The results of this attitude are as pathetic as they are inevitable. *People who don't rest burn out.* Many of those who begin the Christian journey with great enthusiasm and excitement find that they run out of energy and can no longer cope with its demands. They believe that they can keep going through their own stamina and strength and lack either the humility or the insight to realize that they need to renew their strength.

But why do we feel guilty about resting? Why do we have this feeling that it is improper to relax? In my own case, I once held the view that every hour that the good Lord sends is meant to be spent working. Sure, I got a lot of things done. But I got exhausted. And, more important, the quality of my relationship with God suffered. I was squeezing him out of my life. I was so concerned with doing things for God that I ended up not spending time with God. Although I was too busy to notice it, the quality of my spiritual life was suffering. Something was wrong. I was trapped in a cycle of addiction to work. Fortunately, I noticed what was happening and was able to break free from it.

"My soul finds rest in God alone" (Psalm 62:1). Yet most of us are so busy doing things for God that we forget that God wants to do things for us—such as refreshing our faith and renewing our vision of the Christian life. We need to make space for God in our lives. If we don't, we will simply become so busy that we exclude God. If we are so busy that we don't have time to enjoy the radiance of God's presence, we are dishonoring God. It is refreshing to be reminded that God rested after the work of creation and invites us to share in that rest. The command to observe a day of rest (Exodus 20:8–11) is not some optional extra that can be discounted by those with busy lives. It is just as important as other commandments. It is there to force us to make space for God and be renewed by his presence. Left to ourselves, we would simply not do this.

If you feel guilty about resting, as I once did, you will find these thoughts helpful.

* All of us long to serve God and do the things he wants. Now, serving on that church committee, going to that meeting, and writing that article are probably all of use to God. Nobody is denying that. But they are actually of secondary importance. *God wants us to spend quality time with him.* Why are we so obsessed with doing things for God if

they prevent us coming into his presence and focusing on him? If we long to do what God wants, we must make space for him and make sure that godly and churchly activity does not in reality become an obstacle between ourselves and God.

- Think of that famous scene involving Mary, Martha, and Jesus (Luke 10:38–42). Jesus wished to spend time with both these sisters. Mary sat at his feet, listening to him, thrilled to be in his presence. Martha was so distracted by household chores—which could have been done at any time—that she did not spend time with the Lord. For Jesus, that was the thing that really mattered. Each of us has household chores—at home, at business, and so on—that can prevent us from spending quality time with the Lord. What are we going to do about it?

- We want to give of our best to God and serve him to the best of our ability. The quality of our service of God will be severely harmed if we have lost our enthusiasm, energy, and commitment. We owe it to God to renew our commitment, vision, and passion if we are to serve him properly. And how can we do this unless we learn to spend time luxuriating in the presence of God, catching a fresh vision of his glory, radiance, and love?

Yet rest is not something that just happens. It is something we need to *make* happen. Perhaps one of the most puzzling aspects of the Christian faith is that *rest is a matter of discipline.* At first, this seems like one of those paradoxes that baffle us. Yet it expresses a simple truth, so often overlooked, that *we need to make space for rest and refreshment.* Rest does not just happen; it is something we need to plan and prepare. When planning a long journey, the careful traveler builds in periods of rest, knowing that to fail to do so would be to risk loss of concentration, exhaustion, and possible injury or death.

So how can we relax in the presence of God and allow him to refresh and renew us? Perhaps the time has come to hitch a ride with a fellow traveler along the road of faith, and learn from them on this matter . . .

Hitching a Ride: *Susanna Wesley*

Our traveling companion for this part of the journey is Susanna Wesley (1669–1745), a woman of considerable spiritual discernment, who has been eclipsed on account of the fame of two of her sons. Susanna kept a personal spiritual journal, whose entries reveal her as a woman of wide reading, deep thought, and penetrating spiritual insight.

Susanna was born on January 20, 1669, married Samuel Wesley in 1689, and went on to have nineteen children by him. Only ten would survive into adult life. The most famous of those children were, of course, John and Charles, who would go on to become leaders of the evangelical revival within the English church during the eighteenth century. Yet Susanna herself was a woman of great faith and immense piety. Life was not easy for her. Samuel Wesley was frequently in debt, making management of the household difficult and painful. The practical necessities of caring for nineteen children made huge demands on her time. At times, she was exhausted. Yet she managed to take care of her spiritual needs, jotting down her thoughts and prayers in her personal spiritual journal.

The journal is a remarkable piece of writing, in which practical wisdom is set alongside mature spiritual reflection. For example, consider Susanna's musings on the weaknesses of a purely philosophical approach to God:

> O Lord, I understand now that to know you only as a philosopher;
> To have the most sublime and conscious speculations concerning your essence, your attributes, your providence;
> To be able to demonstrate your Being from all or any of the works of nature;
> And to discourse with the greatest elegancy and propriety of words of your existence or operations;
> Will avail us nothing unless at the same time we know you experimentally,
> Unless the heart perceives and knows you to be her supreme good, her only happiness!

For Susanna, it was necessary to *experience* God. Being able to prove God's existence, or speculate concerning his attributes, had little value unless God is known "experimentally"—an older English word meaning "from experience."

It is perhaps not surprising that the theme of rest occurs frequently in that journal. Finding space for God in the midst of a frantically busy and financially challenged life was no easy matter. Yet Susanna believed passionately that the discipline of making space for God in the midst of a hectic life was essential to spiritual stability and personal fulfillment. This is no legalism but simply the recognition of our need to set aside time for reflection, prayer, and worship.

Susanna's personal discipline included the protection of Sunday as a day of rest, in which physical relaxation was accompanied by spiritual refreshment. For Susanna, Sunday was a space that had been created by God for exactly this purpose and was meant to be used joyfully and profitably. The fact that God had set aside a day was a matter of grace as much as law: we are commanded to make use of it because it will be of benefit to our relationship with God.

This is the Day that the Lord hath made; I will rejoice and
    be glad therein
Glory be to Thee, Eternal Father of spirits, for so kindly
    and mercifully indulging one Day in seven
to the souls Thou hast made.
Wherein it is their duty as well as happiness,
to retire from the business and hurry of a tumultuous and
    vexatious world,
and are permitted to enjoy a more immediate and uninter-
    rupted attendance on the Divine Majesty.
Oh Blessed Indulgence! Oh most Happy Day!

Lord I can never sufficiently adore Thy Infinite Love and
    Goodness
in appropriating this seventh part of my time to Thy Self.
May these sacred moments ever be employed in Thy service.
May no vain unnecessary or unprofitable thoughts or dis-
    course ever rob You of Your due honor and praise on
    this Day;

or deprive my soul of the peculiar advantages and blessings
   which are to be gained,
by the conscientious performance of the duties of the Day.

Notice how Susanna sees rest as a "duty as well as happiness," in that she is able to "retire from the business and hurry of a tumultuous and vexatious world," and "enjoy a more immediate and uninterrupted attendance on the Divine Majesty."

Susanna would urge us to discipline ourselves into making space to spend time with God along the road of faith with the utmost seriousness. This is a faithful reflection of a major New Testament theme. For Paul, the Christian life is not simply a journey—it is like a race—a long and arduous journey undertaken under pressure in which the winners receive a crown (see Galatians 2:2; 2 Timothy 4:7). The image is also used in the letter to the Hebrews, which urges its readers to persevere in the race of life by keeping their eyes focused firmly on Jesus (Hebrews 12:1–2). This image allows Paul to stress the importance of discipline in the Christian life.

For Susanna, the implications of this image are clear. The journey of faith requires both physical fitness on the one hand and periods of rest and recovery on the other. Susanna challenges us to get rid of those guilty feelings that lead us to think that rest is a bad and dishonorable thing and recover a more biblical way of thinking, namely, that rest is a discipline that God demands of us in order to deepen our relationship with him.

So many of us feel guilty when we are not doing something with an obvious result—such as clearing our desks of correspondence, working in the garden, doing household chores, or attending church meetings. Yet Susanna reminds us that spending time with God is both a luxury and a necessity, something that is a delight in itself and equips us to serve God better.

Challenged and encouraged by this thought, we prepare to move on to the next stage of our journey.

Chapter 6

The Third Stage

John Bunyan opened his *Pilgrim's Progress* by describing his walk "through the wilderness of this world." As the people of Israel pressed onward through the wilderness, they found it increasingly difficult to maintain their morale. The Promised Land seemed a distant hope. And they had now traveled too far to return to the familiar comforts of Egypt. They were living in a wilderness between two worlds—the past and the future.

It is not an easy situation. We must remember that the Promised Land had never been seen by any of those traveling. It was held before them as the land the Lord had prepared for them. But none of them were really sure that it existed. On the other hand, many could remember Egypt and remained set on returning there. Surely its known comforts were to be preferred to the hardships of the wilderness or the unknown land that was said to lie ahead?

Christians find themselves sharing this tension. Paul assures his readers that they are "citizens of heaven" in much the same way as he was a citizen of the great city of Rome. It is indeed a great privilege to be a citizen of heaven—yet, just as the people of Israel could not be sure that the Promised Land *really* lay ahead, so we sometimes find ourselves wondering if there is a heaven over the horizon of this world.

In the end, we carry on traveling in hope. The same God who called Abraham to leave his native land behind and set out for Canaan (Genesis 12:1–5) has also called us. Abraham chose to trust God and set out in faith. The trustworthiness of God outweighed all other considerations. We, too, have been summoned to and are sustained along the journey of faith by that same faithful Lord. There remain many things we do not understand and others we long to know more about. Yet, in the end, the total trustworthiness of God sustains us along that long and difficult journey.

Perhaps we need to remind ourselves of the trustworthiness of that God and his immense and overflowing love for us. So we turn to consider another landmark that guides us as we travel.

⁂ LANDMARK: REDEMPTION

We are in exile through sin, cut off from our homeland. So is there no hope of return? Are we doomed to remain in this wilderness forever? It is at this point that we turn to consider one of the most thrilling and astonishing themes of the Christian faith—the redemption of the world through Christ. As with all the great landmarks of our faith, it is important that we both understand and appreciate it.

To understand the redemption of the world is no easy matter. Why on earth should God want to redeem people like us? Why should he love us so much? What have we done to deserve so great a gift—something no human achievement could ever attain and no human wealth ever purchase? In one sense, it is impossible to understand why the Son of God loves us and gave himself for us (see Galatians 2:20). *But the simple fact of the matter is that this is exactly what happened.*

Charles Wesley expressed this sense of amazement at the love of God, shown in Christ, in his famous hymn "And Can It Be?"

> 'Tis mystery all! th' Immortal dies!
> Who can explore his strange Design?
> In vain the firstborn Seraph tries
> To sound the Depths of Love divine.
> 'Tis mercy all! Let earth adore;
> Let Angel Minds inquire no more.

The point being made here is that the full extent of the love of God is as incomprehensible as it is *real*—and that we should rejoice at it even if we cannot fully understand it.

The death of Christ on the cross means the end of our exile. The gates of heaven have been thrown open to receive us. Christ's death has secured our citizenship of heaven, and we can rest assured that we shall enter that homeland in triumph for eternity. Our sin has been purged, and our ransom price paid.

Jesus himself declared that he came "to give his life as a ransom for many" (Mark 10:45). Now, a ransom is a price paid to achieve someone's freedom. How does this help us appreciate more the meaning of the death of Christ? To speak of Jesus' death as a "ransom" suggests three ideas.

First, it points to someone being held in bondage—for example, some great public figure held captive against his or her will. Their freedom depends totally upon someone being prepared to pay the ransom demand. Israel was held captive in Egypt and longed to be set free. We are trapped in sin, like prisoners in a dark and gloomy dungeon, and long to be set free and allowed to enter the brilliant world of fresh air and sunlight.

Try to imagine what it is like to be in bondage like this, without any hope of deliverance. The price being demanded for you is very high. Who is going to pay the price to set you free? Who cares for you enough to do that? Unless you really matter to someone, you are going to remain in bondage. And there is nothing you can do about it. The emotional impact of this situation is devastating. You are hopeless and helpless. Unless, that is, someone loves you enough to pay the price to get you out.

This brings us to the *second* idea implied by a ransom—a price that is paid to bring about the freedom of the captive. The more important the person being held to ransom, the greater the price demanded. One of the most astonishing things about the love of God for us is that he was prepared to pay so dearly to set us free. The price of our freedom was the death of his one and only Son (John 3:16). Think about that. How much we must matter to God! As Mrs. Cecil F. Alexander put it in one of her best-known hymns:

There was no other good enough
To pay the price of sin;

> He only could unlock the gate,
> Of heaven, and let us in.

The *third* idea is that the death and resurrection of Jesus are liberating. We are set free! The New Testament reminds us that Jesus has set us free from the fear of death (Hebrews 2:14–15) and brought us into the glorious freedom of the children of God. Charles Wesley expresses this as well in the hymn "And Can It Be?"

> Long my imprisoned Spirit lay,
> Fast bound in Sin and nature's night
> Thine Eye diffused a quickning Ray;
> I woke; the dungeon flamed with light.
> My chains fell off, my heart was free,
> I rose, went forth, and followed Thee.

We have been taken out of captivity and set firmly on the road to glory, with Christ ahead of us as our redeemer and trailblazer. He has set us free and goes before us to prepare the way for us. We are like the people of Israel who have been set free from their captivity in Egypt and begin their long journey to the Promised Land.

Many Christians *understand* that they have been redeemed by Christ but have failed to *appreciate* the enormous implications of this fundamental gospel theme. We must not treat our redemption in Christ simply as an idea that we understand. We need to go deeper—much deeper.

To begin with, we need to stop treating the cross of Christ as just a slogan or theological formula and grasp it as a life-changing event. Clear your mind of every irrelevant thought and begin to focus on Christ dying on the cross, gradually filling in the fine detail around it. Allow the cross to impact on your emotions, not just on your intellect. You may find the following helpful as you do this:

- You are there at Calvary, watching Christ die. You are not just reading an account of his death; you are present at the event itself and experiencing it as a living reality.
- Picture Christ on the cross, his arms outstretched.
- See the wounds inflicted on him by his executioners. Imagine the cruel nails rammed through his hands.
- See his face contorted with agony. It is a sad yet kindly face. He is in great pain and has not long to live.
- Around him, there is a crowd of people making fun of him. There is no one to console him in his final hours. It is a scene perhaps too horrible for many of us to contemplate without being distressed. The Son of God is being put to death in one of the most barbaric ways possible. *And all of this took place for us.*

So how can we be helped to appreciate the wonder of this event? How can we grasp the amazing news that God loves us this much? How can we take to heart the full implications of the cross? It is time to join up with a fellow traveler along the road of faith and spend some time in his company. . . .

Hitching a Ride: **Isaac Watts**

Our traveling companion is justly celebrated as one of the greatest writers of hymns in the English language. Isaac Watts (1674–1748) was born in the southern English city of Southampton and was educated at Stoke Newington, now a suburb of London. Watts was a man of deep faith who realized that the singing of hymns could be a powerful aid to personal devotion. At the time, the use of music in worship was regarded with great suspicion within the rather strict form of Christianity to which Watts belonged. Watts's hymns did much to change those views and pave the way for the widespread use of congregational hymn-singing in the English evangelical revival of the eighteenth century. His best-known hymns include many still sung today, including "When I Survey the Wondrous Cross," "Jesus Shall Reign Where'er the Sun," and "O God, Our Help in Ages Past." Watts was convinced that much of the Christianity of his day was superficial. He longed to go deeper and learn more. His advice to his readers reflects this concern: "Do not hover always on the surface of things, nor take up suddenly, with mere appearances; but penetrate into the depth of matters, as far as your time and circumstances allow." We see this concern to "penetrate into the depth of matters" in his devotional hymns, which stimulate personal devotion through active engagement with their themes.

His best-loved hymn, sung by Christians of all denominations, especially on Good Friday, which is a meditation on the cross, intended to evoke a sense of wonder and commitment on the part of its audience. In "When I Survey the Wondrous Cross," Watts offers a reflection on the cross designed to allow its audience to see the attractions of the world in their proper perspective. In addition to painting a vivid word-picture of the cross, Watts stresses that all else pales in insignificance in its light.

> When I survey the wondrous Cross
> On which the Prince of Glory died,
> My richest gain I count but loss,
> And pour contempt on all my pride.
>
> Forbid it, Lord, that I should boast
> Save in the Cross of Christ my Lord
> All the vain things that charm me most,
> I sacrifice them to his blood
>
> See from his head, his hands, his feet
> Sorrow and love flow mingled down;
> Did e'er such love and sorrow meet?
> Or thorns compose so rich a crown?
>
> Were the whole realm of nature mine,
> That were an offering far too small;
> Love so amazing, so divine,
> Demands my soul, my life, my all.

Note how Watts invites the reader (or singer!) of this hymn to meditate on the cross. The hymn builds up a verbal picture of the cross, focusing attention on the pain experienced by the dying Christ and on the fact that this is the means by which the redemption of the world—including the singer!—has been accomplished. The hymn concludes by emphasizing the need to respond to that cross. There is nothing that can equal in magnitude the offering that was made by Christ. But we can at least try—by offering ourselves to Christ in order that his love might be made known to all.

Watts offers us a powerful stimulus to our personal devotion. As we sing God's praise, we simultaneously build up a picture of the inestimable love of God shown to us in the redemption of the world and gain a new appreciation of its immense costliness to the one who died to redeem us. Our reason and emotion are both engaged as we praise the one who redeemed us. Watts's hymn paints a vivid picture of the cost of redemption to our redeemer and moves us to long to thank him and serve him. It is a powerful source of encouragement to us as we travel.

It is also a challenge to reappraise our priorities and values. Martin Luther once wrote these words: "Whatever your heart clings to and confides in, that is really your God." Have we allowed our career, our finances, or our status to become our God by making these into the things in which we trust and which we constantly think about? Watts's words challenge us:

> Were the whole realm of nature mine,
> That were an offering far too small;
> Love so amazing, so divine,
> Demands my soul, my life, my all.

It is Christ who must be at the center of our lives and thoughts. We all need moments of quiet to reappraise our commitments and priorities and begin to redirect our lives to its foundation and its final goal—Jesus Christ.

So how does Watts encourage us on our journey? One thought that we can take away from our encounter with him will serve us well as we travel. We must keep our hearts and minds focused on Christ. Watts's hymn calls to mind the cost of our redemption and the enormous privilege of being called to share in the journey of faith. So often we see it as a burden; in reality, it is a privilege. Our Lord has already been through whatever pain and sorrow we know and experience along the way. He knows and understands what we are going through. He has been there himself. And—amazingly!—he chose to die so that we might follow in his footsteps and enter into his glorious kingdom to be with him forever.

And so we continue on our way through the wilderness, perhaps singing one of Watts's hymns with him as we journey. There are many obstacles that lie ahead—yet Watts's hymns help us focus on the Lord who has redeemed us and will sustain and support us as we travel.

WILDERNESS: FEAR

Traveling through the wilderness is a difficult experience and gives rise to a range of emotions. We feel tired; we long to arrive at our destination. Yet there is another wilderness emotion that many experience on the journey of faith—fear.

Scripture encourages us to fear the Lord. Once that is done, there is nothing else that need be feared. It is true that we will encounter many things that dismay and discourage us along the road of faith. Yet we must grasp that once we have been firmly embraced by the Lord, we are safe. He has called us to travel along the road, and he will uphold and defend us along the way.

As Israel trudged through the wilderness on the way to the Promised Land, it was promised rest and safety once its traveling days were over (Deuteronomy 12:10):

> *You will cross the Jordan and settle in the land the Lord your God is giving you as an inheritance, and he will give you rest from your enemies around you so that you will live in safety.*

The words spoken to the returning exiles from Babylon speak to us as well (Isaiah 43:1–2).

> Fear not, for I have redeemed you;
> I have summoned you by name; you are mine.
> When you pass through the waters, I will be with you.
> And when you pass through the rivers, they will not sweep
>   over you.

We need to pause and savor these words and the promises they convey.

How do we know that we can trust God? This question recurs throughout the journey. Indeed, one of the fears that many Christians secretly experience is that God may have forgotten us, or that his promises cannot be trusted. It is vital that this fear is addressed.

Why do we fear that we cannot trust God? Perhaps part of the problem is our deep-rooted fear that we will be disappointed. We are so used to being let down. Might not God do the same? This fear needs to be confronted. The Old Testament sets out the great promises made to Israel as it traveled through the wilderness. God would lead it to the Promised Land. Try to project yourself into the situation:

- ❧ You are traveling through the wilderness.
- ❧ You are told that there is a promised land flowing with milk and honey ahead.
- ❧ You have been on the road for many years, and all you can remember is the bleakness of the wilderness, the rocky paths, and the pain of hunger. There is no sign of any lush and fertile land ahead.

It must have been difficult for Israel to believe the promises of what lay ahead. But we know something that Israel could not know for certain as it traveled—that there *was* a promised land, and that it *did* enter it. We share their doubts and fears as it travels—but can look ahead and see that these fears were ground-less.

We need to apply that insight to our own situation. We sometimes wonder if there really is a New Jerusalem beyond the horizons of this life. We have been promised it. But is it really there? We can rest assured that the sense of relief experienced by Israel when it saw the Promised Land ahead can be ours—because we trust in the same totally trustworthy God.

Yet perhaps the greatest fear we experience along the journey concerns its ending. Does the journey of faith simply end with death—or is there something beyond, as we passionately believe and hope? There comes a moment in the life of just about all human beings when terrifying thoughts of death flash through their minds, often late at night. Many realize that they simply cannot cope with them.

Very often, the death of a close friend or relative proves to be a turning point in people's lives, often leading to the birth of faith, as they realize that death is an issue that cannot be avoided forever. It has to be faced up to. And many discover that they just cannot cope with the awful reality of death. Many people are secret prisoners of the fear of death. They devise all sorts of coping mechanisms to allow them to live without having to confront the fact that one day they will die. Most modern Westerners seem to spend a lot of their time working out ways of denying their mortality. Death is always something that happens to someone else.

The cross liberates us from the fear of death. It acts as a powerful antidote to our natural tendency to be frightened or anxious about our situation in the world. It allows us to face death with a quiet and calm confidence, knowing that its sting has been drawn by the cross and victory given through the resurrection. Paul's letter to the Hebrews makes this point powerfully when it declares that Jesus died in order that he might "free all those who all their lives long have been held in slavery by their fear of death" (Hebrews 2:14–15).

Now notice what this approach is saying. It isn't saying "Let's pretend that death has been defeated. Let's pretend that its power has been broken. And let's live our lives as if death should not worry us." That would be like closing our eyes to the harsh realities of life and living in a world of fantasy—like stepping into a fairy tale, or into a game of Dungeons and Dragons.

No! Through the cross and resurrection of Jesus Christ, the power of death has been broken. We have been given victory over death through Christ. And that knowledge ought to change us. It ought to transform the way we think and the way we live. We need not fear death anymore, because on the cross, Christ grappled with it and defeated it. This is no imaginary world of an overexcited and fertile human imagination. It is the real world of the gospel, given and guaranteed by God himself.

The cross liberates us from this malignant tyranny of death. It breaks its oppressive stranglehold over us. The New Testament resonates with the joyful realization that Christ lives—and that, because he lives, we shall live also. Christ's victory over the power and reality of death is our victory. Faith unites us to Christ and all that he has achieved, including the defeat of death through death. It is true that in the midst of life, we are in death. But it is even more true that in the midst of death, we are in life—the eternal life made available to us through the gospel, which nothing—not even death itself—can take away from us. "Death has been swallowed up in victory" (I Corinthians 15:54).

The time has come to hitch another ride through the wilderness. . . .

Hitching a Ride: *John Bunyan*

Our traveling companion in what he referred to as "the wilderness of this world" is John Bunyan (1626–88), perhaps one of the best-known Puritan writers of the seventeenth century. Bunyan was born in the English county of Bedfordshire and became involved with the Puritan cause during the English civil war. With the establishment of the Puritan commonwealth, Bunyan turned his attention to preaching and became the minister of an independent congregation in Bedford. His Puritan sympathies caused him to be out of favor when the English monarchy was restored in 1660, with the result that he spent many years inside the Bedford jail.

Bunyan used his time in jail well. One of the works dating from this period is his autobiography, *Grace Abounding to the Chief of Sinners*. Bunyan's best-known work is *The Pilgrim's Progress*, the first part of which appeared in 1678, and the second in 1684. The book has become one of the best-loved works of English religious literature. It sets out to recount the journey of Christian from the "city of destruction" to the "heavenly city," and offers a vivid account of the various spiritual trials and temptations faced by believers as they live out their faith in a frequently hostile world.

In the second part of *The Pilgrim's Progress*, Bunyan relates the story of a group of travelers along the "King's Highway," including Mr. Great-Heart. Their progress along this highway was hindered by their fear of the fierce lions who are known to lie ahead.

> *So they went on, till they came within sight of the Lions. Now, Mr. Great-Heart was a strong man, so he was not afraid of a Lion; but yet, when they were come up to the place where the Lions were, the boys that went before were glad to cringe behind, for they were afraid of the Lions.*

Mr. Great-Heart drew his sword, knowing that a difficult struggle lay ahead. The highway at this point was overgrown with grass, a sure sign that nobody had passed this way for some time. In the event, Mr. Great-Heart was able to overcome the owner of the lions. As he prepares to deal with the lions themselves, he notices something. As Bunyan put it:

The Lions were chained, and so of themselves can do nothing.

In other words, the lions' freedom was limited. They remained fierce; they retained their ability to devour and destroy. But they could not grasp their victims, who remained safely beyond their reach.

What point was Bunyan making through the allegory at this point? The simplest explanation of this part of the story is that the lions represent the great enemies of faith, such as death, sin, and Satan. These continue to be fearful presences along the road of faith. *But they have been chained.* Someone has been along the road of faith ahead of us and has fought these enemies of faith on our behalf. Whoever has been ahead has neutralized the threat they pose. They may frighten us—but they cannot harm us. They are lions that may roar at us but cannot devour us. It seems that Bunyan is working with the classic idea that Christ has dealt with the power of death, sin, and Satan, even though they remain present along the road of faith. *We need not fear them.* Their sting has been drawn.

So how does Bunyan encourage us as we journey along the King's Highway of faith? He reminds us that we will encounter many things that will frighten us and seem to make that journey impossible. Yet we need to trust that their power has been neutralized through the saving death and resurrection of Jesus. They are like the strong man who has been tied up by someone stronger than himself (Matthew 12:29).

Charles Wesley expressed a very similar thought in his well-known hymn "Love's Redeeming Work Is Done":

Lives again our glorious King!
Where, O death, is now thy sting?
Dying once, he all doth save.
Where thy victory, O grave?

Armed with this insight, we can cope with the fears we face along the road of faith. Though we encounter fearful obstacles, we journey in hope.

⊛ OASIS: FELLOWSHIP

Life on the road can be hard and discouraging. *Yet it is not a journey we need undertake on our own.* Part of God's gracious provision is fellow travelers along that road of faith. They are there to refresh us, to build us up, and to encourage us as we travel together to the New Jerusalem. Fellowship is not a luxury we can dispense with or should feel guilty about. It is a spiritual necessity vital to our spiritual growth. God has not created us to be alone but to exist and develop in relationship with others.

At its heart, fellowship is about sharing. The Greek word *koinonia*, used extensively in the New Testament, can bear various senses, including "having in common" and "participating." The fundamental idea is that the believer has fellowship both with Christ on the one hand and with other believers on the other—and that the latter is a means of deepening the former. So how can this be? Why is fellowship of such importance to spiritual growth? Why is company on the journey preferable to solitude?

John Wesley once commented that "there is nothing more unChristian than a solitary Christian." At first sight, this might seem something of an overstatement. After all, surely there is a place for solitude in the Christian walk of faith? Being alone allows us to pray and reflect. Did not Jesus himself withdraw from the company of his disciples in order to pray? A little isolation along the journey allows us space to reflect.

Yet there is all the difference in the world between short periods of solitude that we have chosen to create and a permanent loneliness that has forced upon us. *Fellowship is the normal, and solitude the occasional, means of growth.* Long periods of loneliness along the road of faith can lead to depression, discouragement, and introversion. The Bible constantly portrays people of faith as members of a community. Sometimes that community is static, as in the case of a great city, or a family on an estate in the countryside. At other points, the community is on the move, as with the people of Israel making their way slowly and painfully through the wilderness. Yet the same principle can be seen in operation: *faith is nourished and supported in community.*

One of the major themes of this book has been the importance of keeping company with other Christians. Our traveling companions have been people whose books can enlighten and enliven our walk of faith. Yet there is another category of people who can deepen our faith—*living believers who accompany us both physically and spiritually.*

Fellowship is to be seen both as a divine gift, reflecting God's gracious support to us throughout our walk of faith, and as our responsibility, reflecting the significant role we can play in supporting, nourishing, and encouraging others—as they will encourage us. The following points are helpful as we enumerate the benefits and privileges of fellowship:

1. The church is the "body of Christ," made up of different members (I Corinthians 12:12–31). Each member has a different role; each is essential, in some way, to the smooth working of the body as a whole. You may not be an ear or an eye—but somebody else is. You may not be very good at administration—but others are. Realizing that the Christian life is corporate enables us to recognize our weaknesses without guilt. The whole body will not die because we are not good at administration. Someone else has that gift and can do it. The important thing is that we all recognize our gifts and ensure that we exercise them within the church. As a result, we all benefit from the gifts of others, and our own weaknesses can be covered through the strengths of others. "Each member belongs to all the others" (Romans 5).

2. This means that we *benefit from the gifts of others.* Fellowship is not simply about giving; it is about receiving. Each who has a gift is invited to use it so that others may share in the rich spiritual endowment that God bestows upon the community of faith as a whole (I Peter 4:10). Paul reminds his readers that spiritual gifts are given for the "edification" or the "building up" of the church (I Corinthians 14:4–5, 12–17). They are not there for amusement or some kind of spiritual thrill. They have a deadly serious function— the strengthening of the body of Christ for service in the world. It is important that we develop a sense of expecta-

tion that God will do great things in and through our
sisters and brothers in faith, and rejoice when others flour-
ish. For when one part of the body flourishes, we all share
in the renewal this brings.

The practical outworking of these themes is of immense importance. Some of the more obvious ways in which they can be put
into practice along the road of faith are set out below:

1. *We are encouraged to share our hard-won insights.* Many of us find
   aspects of our faith puzzling and long to have light shed
   on them. There will be many who are fellow travelers on
   the road who will have given long and careful thought to
   these matters and may be able to help us make sense of
   what is presently puzzling us.
2. *We are encouraged to share our personal stories.* All travelers on the
   journey has a story to tell. The story will recount how they
   came to be on that road, the hardships and encouragements
   they have experienced to date, and their hopes for the
   future. Listening to others tell of how they came to faith
   and grew in grace can be immensely encouraging to others.
   We need to share what God has done and continues to do
   in our lives. In the Middle Ages, Geoffrey Chaucer wrote
   The Canterbury Tales, a rather salacious collection of stories
   told by pilgrims as they journeyed to Canterbury. We can
   tell each other uplifting and encouraging stories of faith
   and take heart from them as we travel.
3. *We are encouraged to take care of each other.* Many get tired as they
   travel and need support. Those who are strong today may
   be weak tomorrow. We must learn to uphold each other

and never to be too proud to accept help when it is offered and clearly needed.

4. *We are invited to pray for one another.* It is immensely encouraging to know that we are being held up before God by others who care for us. Praying for others encourages us to identify their needs.

5. *We are asked to confess to one another.* One of the most interesting aspects of the letter of James is the importance it attaches to prayer for each other. James asks us to "confess our sins to each other and pray for each other" (James 5:16). Sin can easily isolate us from others and, above all, from God. The more isolated someone becomes, the greater the grip that sin can hold on his or her life. Being encouraged to confess our sins to one another prevents us from becoming isolated and suffering the loneliness that can lead to depression. It also helps us turn and confess those sins to the one who really matters—our Lord and Savior.

All these are of major importance. We encourage others, and others encourage us. Together, we can press on toward the goal of our journey, encouraging one another as we travel. Yet there is another aspect of fellowship we must consider. This relates to our need to learn humility. Paul states this matter very clearly (Philippians 2:3–4):

> Do nothing out of selfish ambition or vain conceit,
> but in humility count others better than yourselves.
> Each of you should look not only to your own
> interests, but also to the interests of others.

Fellowship helps us to learn humility. This is no easy lesson, as our instinct is to think of ourselves as being better than others. Paul demands—rightly!—that we abandon such kinds of thinking.

We must learn to see others as Christ sees them.

This is not always easy. We must purposefully see in each of our traveling companions a person for whom our Lord died. We may not have a high regard for him or her. Christ sees things in a different light. We must learn to share Christ's estimation of others. This may involve us deliberately choosing to seek and name the gifts and graces of others and by doing so realize that they have many good points to which we were previously blind. The quality of fellowship is thus perceptibly deepened.

It is fatally easy to write others off, to dismiss them as insignificant. Yet this is a secular, not a Christian, way of thinking. One of the tasks we must set ourselves as we journey is to abandon the standards of this fallen and wayward world and begin to anticipate the standards of the New Jerusalem. We do not need to wait before we enter the portals of the heavenly city before we start behaving and thinking according to its norms.

As we draw nearer to journey's end, we once more prepare to be encouraged by another traveler along the road to the New Jerusalem. And so we prepare to hitch a ride and spend time in the company of another of God's pilgrim people. . . .

Hitching a Ride: **Dietrich Bonhoeffer**

We hitch a ride with a German Lutheran pastor who was executed by the Nazis during the Second World War. Dietrich Bonhoeffer (1906–45) was born in Breslau and grew up in the

German capital, Berlin. He became interested in Christian theology at an early age and completed his doctorate in theology at the remarkably young age of twenty-one. He was deeply disturbed by the Nazi rise to power in Germany in 1933, which seemed to him to threaten to destroy authentic Christianity within Germany.

In 1935, he was invited to take charge of a rather unusual seminary. This would be a seminary that operated in secret within Germany, hiding its existence from the Nazi authorities. For several years, Bonhoeffer lived with about twenty-five seminarians, aiming to maintain faithfulness to biblical ethical and spiritual insights at an increasingly tense period in German history. It was during this period that Bonhoeffer put together the material that can be found in his two best-known books, *Life Together* and *The Cost of Discipleship*.

When the Second World War broke out, Bonhoeffer attempted to maintain his ministry. He traveled around Germany, speaking and preaching in secret for the Confessing Church. It could not last; he was a wanted man. He was arrested in April 1943 and executed by hanging on April 8, 1945. This was a Sunday. A few minutes before he was taken away to be executed, he had preached to the inmates at the Flossenberg concentration camp. The text on which he preached was Isaiah 53:5: "by his wounds we are healed."

In *Life Together*, Bonhoeffer brings out the privileges and benefits of Christian fellowship and community. The points he makes were of especial importance to German believers during the oppression of the Nazi period; nevertheless, they remain important to us today. Bonhoeffer stresses that the Christian life tends not to be led "in the seclusion of a cloistered life"; rather, it is lived out "in the thick of foes." In other words, the place in which we are called to live and witness as Christians is *the world*—a hostile place. We might prefer, as Bonhoeffer dryly comments, to "sit among lilies and roses"; yet the demands of Christian witness call us away from such security. We are called to be scattered throughout the world as the people of God (Zechariah 10:9).

Bonhoeffer stresses both the "curse and the promise" of this situation. It is a *curse* in that the people of God are dispersed, and can easily become isolated and despondent. On the other hand, it is a *promise* in that it means that the people of God are present in every place and can be seeds for the growth of the Christian faith in those regions that would otherwise never have heard of Christ and his gospel.

Bonhoeffer locates the importance of Christian community in *affirming the promise and blunting the curse.* Fellowship supports and sustains the people of God as exiles in a distant country, far from their homeland. And that same fellowship provides them with the reassurance and encouragement they need to sow the seeds of the gospel in that distant land. They know that they are not on their own.

Bonhoeffer is clear that not all Christians enjoy such fellowship. Those who are imprisoned or who proclaim the gospel in heathen lands know little of the comfort of the physical presence of other believers. Bonhoeffer regards John, who was exiled on the island of Patmos, as an excellent example of a lonely figure who found consolation in a specific form of fellowship—the visionary contemplation of the worship of heaven and the calling to mind of the worship of other churches whose fellowship he had known.

So what do we take away from the time shared with Dietrich

Bonhoeffer along the road of faith? Perhaps we need to realize how precious is the privilege of Christian fellowship. We need that support and comfort as we travel and try to plant the seeds of the gospel in the lands through which we pass. Bonhoeffer urges us never to take this privilege for granted and to value the presence and contribution of others. When times get tough, we can bear each other's burdens and help each other along the rugged road of the kingdom.

Yet there is more to Bonhoeffer's insight than this. It is a wonderful thing that many have traveled the road of faith before us and that others are making that same journey with us now. It is excellent that we can share our burdens and our joys and that we can learn from one another. But there is another thought we must cherish as one of the chief wonders of the Christian gospel. *We shall meet again!* One day, we shall be united with our fellow travelers—past, present, and future—in the New Jerusalem, secure from our enemies and delivered from sin, death, and suffering. There will be a reunion of those who have journeyed.

It is impossible to avoid being excited by this thought. And, encouraged by it, we bid farewell to our traveling companion and prepare to move onward—knowing that we shall meet him again in the New Jerusalem.

Chapter 7

The Fourth Stage

We are nearing the end of our journey. After persevering for so long, our hopes are rising. We know that the mountains are there in the distance and that from them we may be able to catch a glimpse of the Promised Land. Like Moses, we long to climb up that mountain and look over to see the land beyond. We want to hear those words of the Lord, but this time spoken to us (Exodus 34:4):

> *This is the land I promised on oath to Abraham, Isaac, and Jacob, when I said, "I will give it to your descendants." I have let you see it with your eyes.*

This was the moment when Moses *knew* that the land he had never seen but in which he had placed his trust *was really there,* stretching away as far as the eye could see. *Imagine how he must have felt!* Moses would never enter that land himself, but he died knowing that God's promises could be trusted and that others would enter into the promised inheritance of the people of God. He now *knew* what he had hitherto *believed*—that he had put his trust in a trustworthy God and in the promises of a God who could be relied upon.

Something very similar happened with Simeon, an old man who, we are told, longed for the "consolation of Israel." Would God ever come and redeem his people as he had promised of old? Had God forgotten his people? When his tired old eyes saw the child Jesus, he knew he could die in peace. God's promises had been fulfilled (Luke 2:25–32).

We long for the reassurance given to Moses and Simeon. We want to be sure that the Promised Land is really there. We want to know that we can trust God. We want our doubts to be vanquished and thrown to one side. Yet we have to learn to live with them without letting them drag us down. Thinking of Israel's long journey from Egypt to the Promised Land can, however, console us. Nobody making that journey really knew that there was a promised land. They had to take it on trust and keep pressing onward. What they were being promised outweighed all the weariness of the journey there. What Moses saw from the mountaintop confirmed both the existence of that land and—perhaps more important—the promises of the God who had led his people to its borders and would then take them across the Jordan River to possess it.

We are promised eternal life in the New Jerusalem. We have never seen its gates or walls. We can hardly imagine what it will be like. Yet this New Jerusalem is held before us as the Promised

Land was to Israel. We need to trust that it is there and begin to anticipate our delight in entering it.

And so we turn to consider our final landmark on the journey—the Christian hope of the final consummation.

❧ LANDMARK: CONSUMMATION

The great Christian hope could be summed up in one word—*consummation*. All things will finally be brought to their glorious conclusion as God brings an end to the universe as we know it and ushers in a new heaven and a new earth. Yet it is not enough to simply understand this. Some Christians seem to think that agreeing that the New Jerusalem awaits us is enough to keep them going. Perhaps it is—for some. But we impoverish our faith unless we allow our hearts, as well as our minds, to anticipate the wonder of entering into the kingdom.

Just as Moses was allowed to see the Promised Land from a distance, so we need to climb our Mount Nebo and allow our minds and hearts to exult at what lies beyond. Beyond the horizons of our vision lies a land that has been promised to us as it was to our forebears. They have passed over the river and entered into its joys. What we can do is to rest assured that this land exists and that it is the most beautiful of all worlds. Faith, as we are reminded, is "being sure of what we hope of, and certain of what we do not see" (Hebrews 11:1).

Imagine that you are Moses. You have been on the road for forty years, leading your people to a land you have never seen. You trusted that it was there but did not know. Maybe you doubted along the road, in the secrecy of your heart. Perhaps it was too good to be true? Then you climb Mount Nebo—and you see a fair and fertile land ahead, bathed in a gentle mist. *Now you know it is for real.* Up to now, you had trusted; now you know. Can you imagine the emotional impact of that sight? The sense of exhilaration mingled with relief?

We need to believe and embrace as a certainty that our promised land, our New Jerusalem, lies beyond the borders of our earthly lives, and live out that life in the sure and certain knowledge that our promised land lies before us, awaiting our entrance.

This point was well understood during the Middle Ages. Many of the great spiritual writers of the period knew that they needed to get their readers to enter into the biblical text and anticipate the experience of entering the New Jerusalem. One of the most important such writers was Bernard of Cluny (c. 1100– c. 1150), who used powerful visual imagery to stimulate reflection on the consummation. One of his best-known hymns is entitled "Jerusalem the Golden":

Jerusalem the golden
With milk and honey blessed,
Beneath thy contemplation
Sink heart and voice oppressed.
I know not, O, I know not
What joys await us there,
What radiancy of glory
What bliss beyond compare.

O sweet and blessed country
The home of God's elect!

O sweet and blessed country
That eager hearts expect!
Jesu, in mercy bring us
To that dear land of rest;
Who art, with God the Father,
And Spirit, ever blessed.

Notice how Bernard draws a parallel between the New Jerusalem and the Promised Land through the imagery of milk and honey. Bernard makes the point that human language is simply not capable of expressing the delight and joy of those who enter this land. As the hymn proceeds, he tries to get his readers to imagine that they are in the city and experiencing the bliss, peace, and rest it brings.

If you are making a long journey to see someone you love, the goal of your journey is going to have a major effect on your behavior. The goal is what motivates the journey in the first place. That goal doesn't stop you pulling over to the side of the road if you see someone get hurt. Nor does it mean that you treat the wonderful people you meet along the way with contempt or pay no attention to the beauty of the country you are driving through. All these things are appreciated but are seen in their context. Wonderful though they may be, journey's end is even more sublime. Allowing our thoughts to dwell dreamily upon our future hope reaffirms its reality and increases our sense of longing to be there and enter into its fullness.

Life on earth can be transformed by the hope of life in the New Jerusalem. And how can it be transformed? By beginning to think about that New Jerusalem and setting our hearts firmly on the great hope of gaining its security and joy. Why are so many

Christians frightened that "they will be so heavenly minded that they are no earthly use"? Allowing our hearts and minds to dwell on our future destiny is *essential* if we are to gain the right perspective on where we are and keep us going.

The poet Frederick Langbridge (1849–1923) expresses this point perfectly:

> Two men look out through the same bars:
> One sees the mud, and one the stars.

Langbridge asks us to imagine two people in prison, looking out through the same window. Although they share the same vantage point, they nevertheless see very different things. The point that Langbridge makes is that some people see nothing but the rut of everyday life, ending in death, while others raise their eyes to heaven, knowing that their ultimate destiny lies with God. Their situation is identical; their outlooks are totally different. They see the same things but from a very different perspective.

We are in exile on earth. Looking upward reminds us that we are looking forward to our redemption, to the savior who will come from heaven (Philippians 3:20) and bring us home with him. To look upward is to remember our homeland and recall the hope of final return. To look downward is simply to allow our weary minds to dwell on the misery of exile and lose sight of the hope that is set before us. So *remember* that Christ has died and is risen! And *anticipate* being with him forever in the heavenly city! We must keep that hope alive as we journey and never allow ourselves to be trapped in the hopelessness of those who believe that life is a rut ending in a grave. The truth is very different— and much more exciting.

Paul asks his readers to keep their thoughts focused on heaven, knowing that Christ has gone there before them and awaits their arrival (Colossians 3:1–2):

Since, then, you have been raised with Christ, set your hearts on things above, where Christ is seated at the right hand of God. Set your minds on things above, not on earthly things.

We need to lock our hopes onto the future rather than allow them to become too heavily entangled with the temporary realities of this fading world. Notice how Paul invites his readers to "set their hearts on things above." He is not asking them merely to think of them or see them as present in their minds. He is asking that they set their affections and ground their hopes upon those heavenly realities.

Our Lord himself spoke along similar lines, and his words need to be given great emphasis (Matthew 5:19–21).

Do not store up for yourselves treasures on earth, where moth and rust destroy, and where thieves break in and steal. But store up for yourselves treasures in heaven, where moth and rust do not destroy, and where thieves do not break in and steal. For where your treasure is, there your heart will be also.

Our Lord's words do more than remind us of our need to set our minds and hearts on the future glory; they offer us a means of checking whether we have, in fact, done so. For if our hearts are preoccupied with earthly things, then we have failed to allow the gospel hope to saturate our lives and thought. As Martin Luther put this point: "Whatever your heart clings to and confides in, that is really your God."

So is our heart really set on our future glory? Or are we locked into earthly things that prevent us from grasping and claiming as our own the great gospel promises of heaven?

These questions pose a powerful challenge to our way of thinking and the values that implicitly shape our lives. Many of us, perhaps without realizing, have failed to allow the hope of glory to mold our thinking and have taken on board worldly values based on a philosophy that could be summarized as "let us eat and drink, for tomorrow we die" (I Corinthians 15:32).

So how are we to regain this glory-centeredness? Perhaps we need to allow someone else to help us as we travel. So we prepare to join company with a fellow traveler who may encourage us and teach us as we continue on the road to the New Jerusalem. . . .

Hitching a Ride: *John Stott*

Our traveling companion is John Stott, widely respected as one of the most important evangelical spiritual and theological writers of the twentieth century. Stott was born in April 1921, the only son of a leading Harley Street medical specialist. He attended Rugby School, one of England's best-known public schools. It was there that he had a conversion experience through the ministry of E. J. Nash. Stott went on to study at Cambridge University and was ordained into the Church of England in 1945. His first job was that of curate—a kind of assistant minister—at All Souls, Langham Place, in London's West End. Thus began his association with this church, which has lasted throughout the remainder of his remarkable ministry.

Stott's contribution to contemporary Christianity has been substantial, not least through his development of the "guest service"—that is, a form of worship particularly suited to the needs of inquirers and seekers. He was heavily involved in student Christian work and developed a considerable reputation as a writer, in particular through his introductory book, *Basic Christianity*. His regular preaching ministry at All Souls led to that church becoming the nucleus of a worldwide group of Christians who looked to Stott for guidance and inspiration concerning the effective communication and preaching of the Christian faith.

There is much to learn from Stott as he accompanies us along the road of faith. Stott has challenged and encouraged his fellow Christians in many ways, not least in his challenge to allow their faith to affect the way in which they think about life. One area of particular interest relates to the way in which the hope of glory impacts on our present existence. Stott brings out clearly how the hope of future glory illuminates the present. It is this matter we shall explore in what follows.

In a series of addresses given to the InterVarsity Mission Convention at Urbana, Illinois, in 1976, Stott developed the importance of the hope of glory for theology, spirituality, and especially evangelism. His addresses issued a clarion call for the recovery of this leading theme of the Christian faith and its application to every aspect of our present Christian lives.

Lift up your eyes! You are certainly a creature of time, but you are also a child of eternity. You are a citizen of heaven, and an alien and exile on earth, a pilgrim traveling to the celestial city. I read some years ago of a young man who found a five-dollar bill on the street and who "from that time on never lifted his eyes when walking. In the course of years he accumulated 29,516 buttons, 54,172 pins, 12 cents, a bent back, and a miserly disposition." But think what he lost. He couldn't see the radiance of the sunlight, and sheen of the stars, the smile on the faces of his friends, or the blossoms of springtime, for his eyes were in the gutter. There are too many Christians like that. We have important duties on earth, but we must never allow them to preoccupy us in such a way that we forget who we are or where we are going.

Stott encourages us to renew our acquaintance with the glory that awaits us and begin to anticipate its wonder. We are surrounded by a great cloud of witnesses who have entered the gates of the New Jerusalem and are urging us onward to join them (Hebrews 12:1–2). Think of all the great Christians who have lived down the ages—men and women who you admire. *One day you will be with them in the banqueting hall of the New Jerusalem.*

So think of the great Christians whom you admire, who have now passed into the glory of God's kingdom. Perhaps you might include some of those who have been our traveling companions on this journey. Or they might be close friends, family members, or pastors who have helped you along life's journey, allowing you to lean on their shoulders when things got tough. They've already crossed the Jordan. They've already entered into glory. And we shall be with them! They are in the great "cloud of witnesses" who cheer us on, as we do our best to complete the race that is set before us (Hebrews 12:1–2).

And spurred on by that exciting thought, we prepare to travel onward into the wilderness.

❧ WILDERNESS: SUFFERING

Suffering is a classic wilderness experience. All of us go through it at some point. It hurts—but it does more than that. It raises questions and erodes confidence. Why does God allow suffering? Many Christians find themselves going through the wilderness when they experience suffering. Their spiritual lives dry up, and they feel lonely and abandoned. They sense that they are alone in the desert wastelands, with no consolation in sight.

Too often, suffering is treated simply as an intellectual puzzle. How can we achieve a logical reconciliation of the following propositions?

1. God is loving and almighty.
2. There is suffering in the world.

Answers may be given to those questions—good answers. But suffering is more than an intellectual game to be played by philosophers and logicians. It affects our emotions. Many who suffer feel abandoned by God. They feel that their faith has let them down. They feel the pain of confusion and bewilderment. Why should God's children suffer? Why do bad things happen to good people?

There is no easy intellectual or emotional answer to suffering. Nobody has one, whether Christian or atheist. Its meaning remains elusive. For the Christian, there is an answer, but it is not an easy one.

We are asked to trust God totally.

We may not understand where he leads us or why things happen to others or to ourselves. Yet we must reaffirm the total trustworthiness of God and our secure knowledge of his goodness and commitment to us. Remember that Christ died for you; that the Son of God willingly laid down his life for you. Ponder these points.

- His love for you is beyond dispute.
- You matter to him profoundly.
- His Son died so that you might live.

Can we really doubt his commitment to us? Our minds may have difficulty in grasping what is going on and what its purpose might be in God's greater purposes. Yet we can rest assured that he may be trusted even where our reason fails. Trust, it must be recalled, is an act of will. So choose to trust God.

It is beyond doubt that suffering exists and that it hurts and puzzles. Yet it must be seen from the perspective of the great landmark we have just explored—the unshakable hope of the final consummation. Paul clearly has this point in mind when he writes (Romans 8:16–18):

The Spirit himself testifies with our spirit that we are God's children. Now if we are children, then we are heirs—heirs of God, and co-heirs with Christ, if indeed we share in his sufferings in order that we may also share in his glory. I consider that our present sufferings are not worth comparing with the glory that will be revealed in us.

Read these words slowly and assemble the components of Paul's line of thought.

1. We are the children of God and members of God's family. We belong! We matter!
2. One of the privileges of being a member of God's family is being an heir.
3. Christ, the Son of God, is our "co-heir." That is, whatever he inherits from the Father, we shall inherit as well.
4. Christ endured suffering and won glory. Perhaps you might like to meditate a little on the cross and resurrection at this point.
5. So we, too, will inherit suffering in the present and glory in the future. Christ is thus the guarantor of this great hope—that suffering will give way to glory, and that there is no road to glory other than through suffering.
6. This means that suffering is an integral aspect of our faith, something that cannot be avoided and that we must learn to see as a gateway to glory.
7. Finally, Paul stresses that the glory that awaits us will totally eclipse our present suffering. There is no comparison between them. We need to wait—and to hope.

In the previous section, we noted some words of John Stott: "You are a citizen of heaven, and an alien and exile on earth, a pilgrim traveling to the celestial city." Suffering is part of our lot as exiles, just as glory awaits us as returning citizens of the New Jerusalem. It is therefore important to let our minds dwell on the vision of the New Jerusalem set out in the final work of the New

Testament, in which we learn that God's new order will end the suffering and pain of the world and his people (Revelation 21:4):

> *[God] will wipe away every tear from their eyes. There will be no more death or mourning or crying or pain, for the old order of things has passed away.*

If we take our eyes off the Christian hope, suffering dominates our horizons. Keeping our gaze fixed firmly on the New Jerusalem lets suffering be seen in its proper context. Suffering is then seen as:

- a wilderness experience, which will end when we enter that promised land;
- part of the old order of things, which will disappear when the Lord creates the new heaven and the new earth;
- an aspect of our exile, which will cease when we enter our heavenly homeland.

In every case, suffering will give way to rejoicing.

A similar point is made in a visually powerful manner by Psalm 130, which calls upon God from the depths of sorrow and bewilderment. Our exile on earth is here compared to a dark night that will finally give way to the dawn (Psalm 130:6).

> My soul waits for the Lord
> More than watchmen wait for the morning.

Imagine that you are a watchman standing on the city walls of Jerusalem at night. Darkness is a time of danger and uncertainty. An enemy could draw close, unobserved, to the walls of the city. Yet with the coming of dawn, light returns and the watchman can go home to rest. So we need to yearn for the coming of the Lord just as the watchman waited patiently for the dawn. He knew it would come just as we must learn to trust that God's new day will finally dawn, and a new world will be created for us to inhabit.

One of the things that most of us find difficult is entrusting ourselves to God, willingly handing ourselves over to whatever he has in store for us, knowing and trusting that he works for our good, whether we can discern this or not (Romans 8:28). Richard Alleine put this powerfully in the eighteenth century, when he drafted a prayer of commitment for the Methodist covenant service:

> *I am no longer my own, but yours. Put me to what you will, rank me with whom you will; put me to doing, put me to suffering; let me be employed for you or laid aside for you, exalted for you or brought low for you; let me be full, let me be empty; let me have all things, let me have nothing.*

Suffering, then, is an important and challenging aspect of our exile. Yet we are not alone here. Countless other travelers along the road of faith have wrestled with this issue before us. So it is entirely appropriate to think about allowing someone who has already been along that road to help us. And so we prepare to hitch another ride along the road of faith. . . .

Hitching a Ride: **Horatius Bonar**

Our traveling companion this time is Horatius Bonar (1808–89), one of Scotland's leading nineteenth-century pastors and hymn writers, perhaps best known for his hymns "Fill Thou My Life, O Lord My God," and "I Heard the Voice of Jesus Say." Bonar was educated at Edinburgh University and began his preaching ministry in the Scottish Borders in 1833. He was involved in the revivals that began to take root in Scotland from 1837 onward. In 1866, he returned to Edinburgh to begin his ministry at the Chalmers Memorial Chapel and was particularly active in the revival meetings led by D. L. Moody in the Scottish capital in 1873.

Although Bonar's ministry was very successful, he was no stranger to suffering. Five of Bonar's children died in quick succession, leaving a deep impression on him. The issue of the place of suffering in the Christian life was never far from the surface of his thoughts and is frequently addressed in his published works.

One of Bonar's most characteristic thoughts is that suffering is "the family badge" of Christians. While Christians are distinguished by many family resemblances, one stands out above all:

They have one mark more peculiar than any of these. It is truly a family badge: they are all cross-bearers. *This is the unfailing token by which each member may be recognized. They all bear a cross. Nor do they hide it as if ashamed of it. "God forbid that I should boast, save in the cross of our Lord Jesus Christ, by whom the world is crucified to us, and we unto the world." Sometimes it is lighter, and sometimes it is heavier;*

sometimes it has more of shame and suffering, and sometimes less, but still it is upon them.

Suffering, for Bonar, is simply inevitable in this "vale of tears" in which we shall spend our exile. It is an immense consolation to know that others have known it before us, and felt its pain.

The path of sorrow is no unfrequented way. All the saints have trodden it. We can trace their footprints there. It is a comforting, nay, it is cheering to keep this in mind. Were we cast fettered into some low dungeon, would it not be consolation to know that many a martyr had been there before us; would it not be cheering to read their names written with their own hands all round the ancient walls? Such is the solace that we may extract from all suffering, for the furnace into which we are cast has been consecrated by many a saint already.

The image offered by Bonar is important. The footprints of the saints are imprinted on the road of faith ahead of us. In journeying, we are following behind them, sharing their experiences and sorrows, just as we shall finally share their joy at entering through the gates of the heavenly city.

For Bonar, it is essential to keep our experience of suffering firmly illuminated by the Christian hope.

"If we suffer, we shall also reign with him" (2 Timothy 2:12). Of this we are assured. Oneness in suffering here is the pledge of oneness in glory hereafter. The two things are inseparable. His shame is ours on earth; his glory shall be ours in heaven. Therefore let us "rejoice, inasmuch as we

are partakers of Christ's sufferings; that, when his glory shall be revealed, we may be glad also with exceeding joy" (1 Peter 4:13).

The hope of heaven allows us to carry on through the vale of suffering, coping with the hardship of exile, yet knowing that its days are numbered. One day, we shall return home.

We are but as wayfaring men, wandering in the lonely night, who see dimly upon the distant mountain peak the reflection of a sun that never rises here, but which shall never set in the "new heavens" thereafter. And this is enough. It comforts and cheers us on our dark and rugged way.

This is powerful imagery—the distant mountain peak laced with a sunlight we can never fully see, and the Promised Land beyond, on which the sun of God's radiant glory will never set! As we leave Bonar behind, and press onward through the wilderness, we find ourselves consoled by his thoughts. Small wonder that we long to be like Moses, and climb Mount Nebo, so that we might peer over into the land beyond the mountain, promised to us as our homeland.

The thought of that land helps us cope with the hardship of exile, as we continue on our journey. . . .

⊛ OASIS: THE FEAST

An oasis is a place of refreshment at which weary travelers can eat, drink, and rest before continuing on their journey. Those three themes—food, drink, and rest—are integral to the New Testament vision of the kingdom of God.

Our Lord frequently compared the kingdom of God to a feast—perhaps like a great banquet thrown in celebration of a marriage (Luke 14:15–24). When the prodigal son returned to his father (Luke 15:11–24), the father threw a feast in celebration of the safe return of the son who he had believed to be lost. But why should the kingdom of God be like a feast?

To appreciate the richness of this image and the insights it offers into the final goal of our journey, we need to tease out its associations. Again, it is important not simply to *understand* these ideas but to try to enter into the situations they presuppose and experience the emotional aspects of the image. To fail to do this is to needlessly impoverish our appreciation of the Christian hope.

First, the image suggests an abundance of food and drink, which are capable of meeting and satisfying human hunger. A leading theme of the Christian understanding of human nature is that we have been created for fellowship with God and are empty otherwise. Augustine of Hippo (354–430) made this point in his famous prayer to God: "You have made us for yourself, and our hearts are restless until they find their rest in you." To appreciate this fully, we need to imagine that we are famished and longing for food to sustain us. The image of the feast is an affirmation of the graciousness of God. Not only does he provide the basics of life which we need to survive; he provides rich food in superabundance.

Second, the image of a feast suggests the idea of *invitation*. A feast is something to which we have to be invited before we can share in the rejoicing and feasting. Jesus himself ate at table with those whom contemporary Jewish society regarded as social out-casts, making the point that these unfortunate people were wel-comed and accepted into his presence. Feasting is about being wanted and welcomed into the presence of someone of dignity and importance. It is a profoundly affirming matter. We need to imagine our sense of delight—and its impact on our self-esteem!—to be invited to such an important event.

Thirdly, feasting is about *celebration and rejoicing.* A feast is ar-ranged to mark an occasion of importance, such as a wedding, so that all those who know and love those who are to be married may share in and express their joy and delight. The long journey through the wilderness of this world is finally over, and journey's end has been reached. At last we can rest!

Fourthly, a feast is held in honor of someone—someone im-portant. To be invited to the feast is to be asked to come into the presence of this person. The feast we are considering is indeed honoring someone special in that it is the wedding supper of the Lamb of God (Revelation 19:7–9).

Some religions depict life after death as involving loss of per-sonal identity through immersion in the vastness of a cosmic ocean, just as a drop of water loses its identity as it falls into the sea. The Christian gospel offers a radically different hope—that of sitting down with the creator and redeemer of the world, along with the vast company of the redeemed, in joy and delight. It is an image to be treasured and safeguarded even if we find it difficult to find words to describe it.

One of my favorite novels is André Gide's *La Symphonie Pastorale.* The book is set in Switzerland during the 1890s and tells the story of a Protestant pastor who befriends a girl who has been blind from birth. One of the things that interested me about the novel was the way in which the pastor tried to describe to the blind girl such things as the beauty of the scenery around them— the alpine meadows, the brilliant colors of the springtime flowers, and the majesty of the snow-capped mountains. The blue flowers by the river, he remarks, are like the color of the sky. Yet then he realizes that she has never seen the sky and so cannot make sense of the comparison. Throughout the work, he finds himself constantly frustrated by the limits of language to convey the beauty and wonder of the natural world to the girl. But words are the only tools he has at his disposal to try to explain what the real world is like to someone whose eyes have never seen it.

Then a new and somewhat unexpected development occurs. An eye specialist in the nearby city of Lausanne indicates his belief that the girl's condition is operable and that her sight can be restored. After three weeks in the Lausanne clinic, she returns to the pastor's home. She is now able to see and experience for herself the sights he had tried to convey using words alone. "When you gave me back my sight," she said, "my eyes opened on a world more beautiful than I had ever dreamed it could be. Yes, truly, I had never imagined that the daylight was so bright, the air was so brilliant, and the sky was so vast." The pastor's patient yet clumsy words could never adequately describe the world she could now see for herself.

The Promised Land was like that for Israel in the wilderness. Heaven is like that for us. It is like the best things we have ever known or experienced—only better. The Promised Land was to flow with milk and honey, assuring Israel that it would be a rich land of plenty. The people of Israel had never seen it, but they could begin to anticipate it before entering into it. Similarly, our eyes have never seen heaven, and we must rely on words to prepare our hearts and minds for what we shall finally encounter. Those words can never fully describe it or prepare us for it. But, like the Promised Land of old, it is there, waiting for us, and will far surpass our expectations when we finally arrive there.

So how is this hope to be kept alive? Like so many of the great images of the Christian faith, it can so easily become stale. Once we become used to something, it loses its power to excite. The person we once found so fascinating becomes predictable; the book that we simply could not put down because it gripped us so powerfully becomes pedestrian; the movie that was so good that we went to see it three times when it first came out somehow seemed rather tame a year later. Familiarity breeds indifference. That is as true for the Christian hope as it is for anything.

But why? Why this problem with overfamiliarity? Why should we lose a sense of excitement about the New Jerusalem or the great feast being prepared for the wedding of the Lamb? The fault lies with us—and it is to be found firmly and securely in our fallen human nature. Sin affects us so deeply that even the things of God become tarnished, tired, and tedious. So what can be done about it?

We must keep this hope alive. We can do so by keeping the gospel image of the feast turning over in our minds, seeing it from different angles.

- We can see ourselves as peeking over the mountains to catch a glimpse of the Promised Land, knowing that one day we shall feast there with our loved ones.
- We can see a meal shared with dear friends as a glorious foretaste of the banquet prepared for all those who love the Lord, at which he himself will be the guest of honor.

- After a long-distance run or an exhausting football game, we could compare our physical thirst to our longing to be with God forever.

- We can realize that the Lord's Supper—which Christians refer to in different ways—is meant both to recall the Last Supper and look forward to the wedding feast of the Lamb. It is thus about *remembering* the past and *anticipating* the future.

- As we prepare to drift off to sleep at night, we can allow our thoughts to focus on biblical texts or images that reinforce our trust in the Christian hope and excite our longing to be with Christ in the New Jerusalem.

Or we can tell stories that point us to the reality of our heavenly hope and help us to visualize it. At this point, we join up with one of the finest storytellers of the twentieth century, as we prepare to hitch a ride along the final stage of our journey.

Hitching a Ride: C. S. Lewis

Our traveling companion for this final stage of our journey is an Oxford don who took delight in writing for children. C. S. Lewis (1898–1963) was born in Northern Ireland and studied at Oxford University. It was while he was a fellow of Magdalen College that he went through a conversion experience in the summer of 1929. His own description of that conversion, published in his autobiography *Surprised by Joy,* brings out clearly how it was not something he particularly wanted—it was something that *happened* to him:

You must picture me alone in that room at Magdalen, night after night, feeling, whenever my mind lifted even for a second from my work, the steady unrelenting approach of Him whom I so earnestly desired not to meet. That which I greatly feared had at last come upon me. In the Trinity Term of 1929 I gave in, and admitted that God was God, and knelt and prayed: perhaps, that night, the most dejected and reluctant convert in all England. I did not then see what is now the most shining and obvious thing; the divine humility which will accept a convert even on such terms.

Lewis specialized in the study of English literature and went on to become professor of medieval and renaissance literature at Cambridge University.

Although he was a prolific writer, Lewis is probably best remembered for his seven children's stories, gathered together as the Chronicles of Narnia. The first of these was published in 1950 as *The Lion, the Witch, and the Wardrobe.* Its central characters—at least, to begin with—are four middle-class English schoolchildren who have been evacuated to the countryside during the Second World War and end up staying in the rambling old house of a slightly eccentric professor. In the course of exploring the house, they stumble across a wardrobe, which proves to be a gateway to the land of Narnia.

Narnia turns out to be ruled by an evil witch who had seized power some time before and subjected the land to her tyranny. However, there are rumors that the lion Aslan—the true ruler of the country—is on the point of returning—and ending the rule of the witch. The children find themselves drawn into this narrative of redemption, into which the leading themes of the Christian understanding of salvation and consummation are skillfully incorporated.

At one point, the coming reign of Aslan is celebrated with a feast. Lewis describes in detail the rich and tempting food that is set before the children. In reading this section of the work, it is essential to realize that England was suffering appalling deprivation during the war years. The food and drink Lewis describes as being freely available would have been unknown—indeed, would have been unthinkable—to English children at that time. They could only dream of such a wonderful feast; in reality, they would have to cope with very limited amounts of only the most basic foodstuffs, all of which were rigorously rationed.

Try to imagine how an English child who was familiar with only limited amounts of the basic foods would respond to a description of a sumptuous feast. Dishes of which she could only dream would be set out before her eyes. Try to capture the sense of anticipation and longing she would experience. For Lewis, heaven is like that feast, holding the promise of something earth can never provide. At best, it can hint at what lies ahead and create a sense of longing for what we know lies beyond our reach. *Yet it is there, awaiting us!*

As Lewis's Narnia feast utterly surpasses the bleakness and drabness of wartime England, so the New Jerusalem will transcend anything we currently know. We can take great comfort from the thought that heaven is like the best of this world—only better.

And excited by this thought, we continue on our journey, knowing that its end is not that far away. At last we shall see the one who we have longed to meet, face-to-face, for our entire lives. It is perhaps too much for us to take in. The psalmist set out his longing to see God in these familiar words (Psalm 27:4):

> One thing I ask of the Lord,
> This is what I seek;
> That I may dwell in the house of the Lord
> All the days of my life,
> To gaze upon the beauty of the Lord.

What the psalmist longed for all his life will one day be ours— to gaze upon the face of our Lord and savior, as we enter into his house, to dwell in peace forever.

Chapter 8

The Journey

Continues ◆ ◆ ◆

While this book now draws to its close, the journey of faith still goes on. The present work has set out a framework for making sense of that journey, offering insights to sustain us as we travel. Yet that journey is an immensely personal undertaking. Each of us has a different agenda, reflecting our unique identity as God's creation and our special personal relationship with that God.

The very fact that we are individual wayfarers on our way to the heavenly city means that we have needs specific to ourselves, not all of which are shared by others. The company one person finds congenial may be irritating and unhelpful to someone else. It is therefore important that you develop the general approach adopted in this book, taking it further and customizing it to your own particular situation.

For example, you could choose additional traveling companions who will accompany you along your personal journey of faith. Your friends will have discovered works of writers who they find encouraging, helpful, and challenging to their walk of faith. Talk to them, and ask them who they have found to be helpful. There are other traveling companions whom many have found to be profoundly helpful, yet who have not been mentioned in this book, due to lack of space—such as Thomas à Kempis (c. 1380–1471), John Calvin (1509–64), John Wesley (1703–91), or Corrie ten Boom (1892–1983).

You will need to bear in mind here that reading Christian writers is a little like listening to music—there are issues of taste and style involved, so that what your friends find attractive may not turn out to be much use to you. You need to look out for writers who seem to be "on your wavelength," or who "speak to your condition" (to use an old but very useful way of speaking). Once you have found writers like this, stay with them! See them as traveling companions along the road of faith. Where possible, do more than read their writings; read their biographies. This will remind you that they are women and men of faith who lived out the Christian life about which they wrote. You can learn from the challenges they faced, the encouragements they received, and the lessons they learned, often painfully.

You should also realize that each of us faces different wilderness experiences. For many, the wilderness themes dealt with in this book will be relevant and important. Doubt, fear, and failure are issues that most of us have to wrestle with from time to time. Yet there are others that may play an especially important role for some. For example, some Christians find loneliness a particularly difficult issue. How can we cope with solitude? And what spiritual treasures lie hidden beneath its apparently hostile exterior? It may be important to deal with issues such as these in order to progress further along the road of faith.

Yet the same general principles used throughout this work can be applied to the continuation of the journey. Through God's good grace, there are others who have made this journey before us. They have traveled through the wastelands and drunk deeply at the oases. They have shed tears in times of loneliness; they have shouted with joy in moments of refreshment. They can be our companions on the journey to the heavenly city.

Many have read Daniel Defoe's great novel *Robinson Crusoe*. The book is set on a desert island on which Robinson Crusoe has been shipwrecked. He believes he is utterly alone. He begins to face the challenge of loneliness and prepares to cope with all the difficulties he knows must lie ahead. Then something happens that changes his entire perspective on his situation. While walking along the shoreline, he notices a human footprint in the sand. Suddenly, everything is changed. *Someone else is there.* Crusoe is not sure whether to be frightened or delighted!

So often we try to get on with the life of faith as if we were hermits, struggling on our own. Perhaps we are too proud to admit that we need help; more likely, we have simply failed to realize that others are accompanying us. Every step of the long kingdom road has been graced by the presence of others before us and moistened with their tears, whether of joy or sorrow. We may learn from what they have already experienced, just as we may find reassurance in the knowledge that they have been through the wildernesses of this world before us. We may take comfort from the presence of others who even now are making that journey alongside us.

And—finally!—we may rejoice in sure knowledge that one day we shall join them in the New Jerusalem, our journeying finally ended, as we raise our voices together in praise at the glorious sight of our Lord and savior and eat and drink with him in the kingdom of God. The journey will then have ended; something else more wonderful will have begun.

Sources of Citations

---

p. 48
Jonathan Edwards, "The Christian Pilgrim," in *Basic Writings* (New York: New American Library, 1966), 136–37.

pp. 65, 66, 67–68
J. I. Packer, *Knowing God* (Downers Grove, Ill.: InterVarsity Press, 1973), 38–39.

p. 78
The Prayers and Meditations of St. Anselm, translated by Benedicta Ward (Harmondsworth: Penguin Books, 1973), 94–95.

pp. 85, 86
Alexander MacLaren, *Victory in Failure* (New Canaan, Conn.: Keats Publishing, 1980), 10–12.

pp. 92, 93–94
Susanna Wesley, "Devotional Journal"; in Michael D. McMullen (ed.), *Hearts Aflame: Prayers of Susanna, John and Charles Wesley* (London: Triangle Books, 1995), 68, 18, 29.

pp. 103, 104
Isaac Watts, "When I Survey the Wondrous Cross," in *Hymns Ancient and Modern Revised* (London: Clowes, 1922), 85.

p. 110, 111
John Bunyan, *The Pilgrim's Progress* (London: Dent, 1907), 217–18.

pp. 129–30
John Stott, "The Biblical Basis for Declaring God's Glory," in D. M. Howard (ed.), *Declare His Glory Among the Nations* (Downers Grove, Ill.: InterVarsity Press, 1977), 90.

pp. 136, 137, 138
Horatius Bonar, *When God's Children Suffer* (New Canaan, Conn.: Keats Publishing, 1981), 19–20; 113; 121.